I0825493

the HOLY SPIRIT

BILL JOHNSON

the HOLY SPIRIT

Who He Is and Why We Can't Live Without Him

WHITAKER HOUSE

Boldface type in the Scripture quotations indicates the author's emphasis.

The forms *Lord* and *God* (in small caps) in Bible quotations represent the Hebrew name for God *Yahweh* (Jehovah), while *Lord* and *God* normally represent the name *Adonai*, in accordance with the Bible version used.

The Holy Spirit:
Who He Is and Why We Can't Live Without Him

Bill Johnson
https://bjm.org/

ISBN: 979-8-88769-310-1
eBook ISBN: 979-8-88769-311-8
Printed in the United States of America

Whitaker House
1030 Hunt Valley Circle
New Kensington, PA 15068
www.whitakerhouse.com

Library of Congress Cataloging-in-Publication Data
LC record available at https://lccn.loc.gov/2024024768
LC ebook record available at https://lccn.loc.gov/2024024769

1 2 3 4 5 6 7 8 9 10 11 𝘄 31 30 29 28 27 26 25 24

To Carrie Lloyd, my inspiration, my friend

CONTENTS

PART TWO: OUR HELPER

PART THREE: AN OVERFLOW LIFESTYLE

ACKNOWLEDGMENTS

I want to thank Carrie Lloyd, Hosanna Kummer, and Michael Van Tinteren for helping me outline what was needed for this book. And, as always, a special thanks to Pam Spinosi for her editing skills.

1

UNIMAGINABLE NEWS

At one time or another, you have probably imagined what it must have been like to be one of Jesus's disciples. Especially when you consider how they came to follow Him. In the first century, there were no modern ways for people to find good associates. Jesus didn't have a series of recruiting meetings, attended by many possible candidates, where He was able to choose the finest from the crowd to join His ministry team. He didn't collect ten thousand job applications to review and call top candidates in for interviews, then pick the final twelve. The men who became Jesus's apostles were not the cream of the crop in any sense of the phrase. Most of them were culturally mediocre, so that they were, in some ways, the most boring of the batch of biblical figures.

But they *became* the cream of the crop because of *whom* they were following. Jesus personally called each of them to follow Him. And the One who called them by name changed—completely—everything about their identity, purpose, and capacity.

CALLED BY JESUS

There was something life-changing even in the voice of the One who called these disciples to Himself. Here is an account from the book of Matthew about the calling of several of them:

> *Now as Jesus was walking by the Sea of Galilee, He saw two brothers, Simon who was called Peter, and Andrew his brother, casting a net into the sea; for they were fishermen. And He said to them, "Follow Me, and I will make you fishers of men." Immediately they left their nets and followed Him. Going on from there He saw two other brothers, James the son of Zebedee, and John his brother, in the boat with Zebedee their father, mending their nets; and He called them. Immediately they left the boat and their father, and followed Him.*
>
> (Matthew 4:18–22 NASB)

What is it that would pull four men from their occupations, which had been passed down from their fathers, into an unknown journey with a relative stranger? Following always requires leaving something behind. These men left their nets, fathers, and boats. I can't imagine that their decision went over well with their families, as the occupation of fishing required the full attention of all on board. No doubt, this fishing business was to be their inheritance. But they left it all and followed Jesus—with actions that shouted *yes* to their new mission in life.

It's also important to note that Jesus made no promises of success to get them to follow. No guarantees of personal accomplishments or fulfillment of dreams. He didn't even mention the heaven versus hell issue that was at stake. When He gave the invitation to follow, what was already in their hearts, what was previously unrecognized by everyone else, came to the surface in that divine moment: it was their wholehearted commitment to God.

The disciples followed Jesus, indeed. But to where? Wherever He went. Of all the journeys ever taken, this one, more than any other, was not about the destination. It was entirely about the journey itself. *They were with Jesus.*

The disciples recognized that Jesus changed the atmosphere everywhere He was present. No exceptions. Whether He was alone with the Twelve, spending time with individual disciples one-on-one, or standing before thousands, He brought the tangible presence of heaven to earth. He lived the manifestation of the kind of prayer He taught them to pray: *"On earth as it is in heaven"* (Matthew 6:10 NKJV, NASB). And the presence of God—the Holy Spirit—was released whenever He spoke. The John 6:63 principle was at work: *"It is the Spirit who gives life; the flesh profits nothing. The words that I speak to you are spirit, and they are life"* (NKJV). The disciples watched Jesus model what He told them so clearly: "I only say what I hear My Father say; I only do what I see My Father do." (See, for example, John 5:19.) Whether they understood this concept or not, they felt it. And it marked them. Jesus's words became *"spirit"* and *"life."* His words released His presence. And that presence was a life-giving force that changed everything.

A FRONT-ROW SEAT

Imagine being in crowds where everyone is pushing and shoving to get close to Jesus, and yet you have the privilege of being within arm's reach of Him at almost any time of the day or night because He *chose* you. The disciples' sense of personal significance could never have been higher than at that time. But neither do I think they would have had the notion that they somehow had earned or deserved this opportunity. It was so far above what any person who had ever lived had experienced. That included their heroes, like Moses, David, and Isaiah. There was little chance of self-aggrandizement because they lived with a consciousness of the grace they had been given.

And then imagine beholding miracles that had never been seen before—by anyone! The disciples had a front-row seat to the miraculous, heaven's invasion of earth, which operates outside of human logic and reason. That front-row seat gave them the chance to watch both the effect of such miracles on the people receiving them and the destiny of entire family lines altered through one touch or one word from Jesus. It must have been exceedingly wonderful, mind-boggling, and—above all—*inviting*. And as if that weren't enough, the Master then equipped them to do the same. Yes, to do the same astounding miracles and deliverances they saw come from Him. They must have been overwhelmed by the fact that their personal story in ministry had already involved seeing the hand of God manifest in miraculous ways. But the acceleration they were now experiencing, which included their own unqualified participation in the working of miracles, must have stretched their imaginations to the breaking point.

WHAT THEY DIDN'T KNOW THEY KNEW

The apostles' normal life activities of fishing, dealing with public officials, and following a religious routine had all lost their luster. Something had been awakened in them that would never be satisfied by anything other than the Jesus way of life. The Spirit of God resting upon the Son of Man had forever transformed everything. Only Judas Iscariot, who never dealt with the issue he had brought with him into his relationship with Jesus (the love of money), couldn't see beyond the immediate benefit or cost of following the One.

Jesus was a movement in Himself. He hosted the Spirit of God in a way that no king, prophet, or priest had done before Him. The crowds were overwhelmed by His miraculous works, displayed as the ultimate revelation of the Father's heart for His creation. And they were stunned by Jesus's words, confessing they had never heard anything like them: *"For He taught them as one having authority"* (Matthew 7:29 NKJV). It became obvious to them that all the other voices spoke without authority. Those voices were just noise. Ideas. Ineffectual commands. There was no life-changing power in them. The contrast between what the people were now hearing and what they had heard for their entire lives was stunning.

The disciples learned by experience what Jesus was teaching them about His life focus: pleasing the Father. Everything He did and said came from the Father, empowered by the Holy Spirit. They no doubt recognized something was unique about Jesus and the way He taught. But did they realize that this uniqueness was the Holy Spirit? There's no way to know for sure, but I doubt they did.

> ***JESUS WAS A MOVEMENT IN HIMSELF. HE HOSTED THE SPIRIT OF GOD IN A WAY THAT NO KING, PROPHET, OR PRIEST HAD DONE BEFORE HIM.***

THE SHOCK OF A LIFETIME

Multiply my description of the disciples' journey with Jesus by a thousand, and you might begin to get a picture of what they faced when He told them the unimaginable news that *He was leaving them*.

Toward the end of His three and a half years with the Twelve, Jesus brought them a revelation that was almost as far outside the disciples' ability to grasp as were the miracles He performed. Hearing that He was leaving them must have been a shock. But the real challenge came when He said His leaving was *to their advantage*. He easily could have said it was important for Him to leave because He was going to atone for their sins so that they could be born again, and that was the advantage. He might have said He was going to rise from the dead and intercede for them before the Father, and this was to their profit. Both statements would have been absolutely true. But, this time, His focus was on the one gift that was so far beyond all the rest of life itself that nothing else deserved immediate attention. He told them that after He left, He would send them *"the Helper,"* the Holy Spirit:

> *But I tell you the truth, it is to your advantage that I go away; for if I do not go away, the Helper will not come to you; but if I go, I will send Him to you.* (John 16:7 NASB)

To their *"advantage"*? That would be hard to believe if you were one of the disciples, currently within arm's reach of the most amazing Person, God Himself in the flesh, walking the earth. Walking not just anywhere, but in the specific part of the world where you lived. Not since Adam and Eve walked with God in Eden in the cool of the evening had anyone been given the chance at such a practical yet profoundly impactful relationship with God in person. (See Genesis 3:8.) How was it possible that Jesus's sending the Holy Spirit, the Helper, was to their advantage over this Edenic experience?

And yet it was. And if it still seems to us like it would be better to have Jesus on earth in the flesh, then we're missing the main point of what He has made available to us: the One whom we can't live without if we are to live the life that Jesus calls us to. Having the Spirit's abiding, indwelling presence is greater than having Jesus with us in the flesh, within arm's reach.

After Jesus's death and resurrection, the remaining eleven disciples eventually got it. They understood the reality of the Spirit's presence and power in their lives. As a result, they were all willing to suffer great trial, tribulation, and even death because of its value. They were forever marked by their advantage.

OUR ADVANTAGE

One of the meanings of the Greek word translated as *"advantage"* in John 16:7 is "to be profitable."[1] A profit is basically an increase from an investment. Jesus promised the apostles they were about to receive an

1. *Strong's Exhaustive Concordance of the Bible,* G4851, Blue Letter Bible Lexicon, https://www.blueletterbible.org/lexicon/g4851/kjv/tr/0-1/.

increase of their investment of time with Him. It would be an increase of all they had seen, heard, and experienced for the past three-plus years. There has never been a profit or an upgrade equal in significance.

I'm a bit embarrassed to say that, several times in recent months (the most challenging season of my life), I found myself saying or thinking, "God, I don't know what I'm doing. I wish You were here, sitting in that chair across the table from me, so You could tell me what to think and do." This cry for Him was both notable and legitimate. It was as sincere as you can imagine. My awareness of my personal need was also legitimate. But in a strange way, that cry of my heart was very similar to the cries of the Israelites in the wilderness, longing to go back to Egypt. It was a step in the wrong direction. As glorious as it would be to have Jesus sitting with me at my table, the reality is, He *is*. The indwelling Presence is sitting at every table where I sit. My awareness of Him, my conscious attention to all that He has said and is saying, is the very thing that positions me to offer my breath, my life, for eternal purposes. Only in offering myself in that context will I be able to leave a mark on the course of history that truly brings Jesus glory.

"ANOTHER, BUT EXACTLY THE SAME"

In the final week of Jesus's earthly life, He had many closing remarks for His disciples. He explained to them about the Spirit—the Helper, the legal Advocate, the Comforter, the One called alongside to assist them—who was coming to be with them:

> *I will ask the Father, and He will give you another Helper, that He may be with you forever; that is the Spirit of truth, whom the world cannot receive, because it does not see Him or know Him,* ***but you know Him*** *because He abides with you and will be in you.*
>
> (John 14:16–17 NASB)

The Greek word translated *"another"* in this verse indicates "another, but exactly the same." Dick Mills, in one of his brilliant word studies in the *Spirit-Filled Life Bible,* describes the meaning of the term in this way: "One besides Me and in addition to Me but one just like Me. He will do in My absence what I would do if I were physically present with you."[2] The Holy Spirit ensures such exactness of ministry, with no loss whatsoever.

Jesus was letting His disciples know that this Helper, the Holy Spirit, who had been resting upon Him during His entire three and a half years of ministry, was exactly the same as He was, with no variation. Everything the disciples had with Jesus, and everything they loved about Him, they would have with and love about the Holy Spirit. He added that they *already knew Him.* Since they knew Jesus, and the Spirit of God was exactly the same as He was, they knew the Spirit of God as well.

Jesus told them, *"He abides with you and will be in you."* In "phase two" of their life with Jesus (after His return to heaven), the Holy Spirit—the atmosphere of heaven they'd been living in because of Jesus, who is the Spirit's ultimate resting place—would take up residence in them. He would not just be *with* them. He would now be the indwelling presence of God.

Yes, the disciples had enjoyed what no other humans had enjoyed since Adam and Eve in the garden: God within their reach. But now it was going to be God *within* them. Period.

EVERYTHING THE DISCIPLES HAD WITH JESUS, AND EVERYTHING THEY LOVED ABOUT HIM, THEY WOULD HAVE WITH AND LOVE ABOUT THE HOLY SPIRIT.

2. Dick Mills, "Word Wealth for John 14:16," in *NKJV Spirit-Filled Life Bible,* 3rd ed., exec. ed. Jack W. Hayford (Nashville, TN: Thomas Nelson, 1991), 1603.

THE SPIRIT WITHIN US

OUR INHERITANCE

What does it mean to have God within us? I'm sure you are probably like me in that you're thankful just to be born again. When I hear people say they aren't looking for a reward from God, I get it. Especially when we understand that everything we do that's right, that pleases God, came from Him in the first place. Even our faith, without which we cannot please God (see Hebrews 11:6), came from Him. We obviously play a role in responding to and living for God. But that role is made possible by Him. Not only that, but He empowers us in everything. Just the thought of being born again, adopted into God's family, is a gift beyond all comprehension. Yet, as only He can do, Jesus pushes the boundary of our comprehension a bit further by adding that we are heirs of God. We inherit God. Astonishing! God, the all-generous and loving One, has given Himself to us. That is what it means to have God within us. *"And if children, then heirs—**heirs of God and joint heirs with Christ**, if indeed we suffer with Him, that we may also be glorified together"* (Romans 8:17 NKJV). In granting this indescribable gift—the Holy Spirit—described as the *"pledge"* (Ephesians 1:14 NASB) or *"down payment"* (AMPC) of this inheritance, God designates there is more to come! He not only gives forgiveness, mercy, grace, blessings, promises, and spiritual gifts galore. He gives us *Himself.*

And here's another astonishing truth: God inherits *us*! *"I pray that the eyes of your heart may be enlightened, so that you will know what is the hope of His calling, what are the riches of the glory of **His inheritance in the saints**"* (Ephesians 1:18 NASB). The first chapter of Ephesians is probably the most mind-boggling chapter in the whole Bible for me. And this thought about God inheriting us is on the top of the pile of thoughts revealed there that are beyond our ability to fully comprehend.

We are not some token part of God's creation. We are not His hobby or a side interest. Humanity is not what He dabbles in on the weekends. *We are it.* We are the crowning touch of His creation, which went bad, but which He spent all to redeem. He is "all in"—to the point that He is what we inherit, and we are His inheritance.

THE SEAL

The Spirit of God is also the seal upon us that designates us as adopted by God. A *seal* is a mark of ownership upon something that secures its contents. I once heard a beautiful story about a businessman from earlier times who would go out to buy grain. He would carry a staff with a seal attached to the end of it, and he would stamp with this seal each bag he planned to purchase. Then he paid for everything and went home to let his workers know how many bags they were to pick up and bring back. The workers knew which bags of grain belonged to their employer because they were the bags that had the mark of the employer's seal (brand) on them. There will be a time when Jesus returns to take home those who are His. It will be evident by the seal of His presence upon the life of believers that they belong to Him.

> *In Him, you also, after listening to the message of truth, the gospel of your salvation—having also believed, you were sealed in Him with the Holy Spirit of promise, who is given as a pledge of our inheritance, with a view to the redemption of God's own possession, to the praise of His glory.* (Ephesians 1:13–14 NASB)

We see that this seal of the Holy Spirit is God's mark of ownership and, again, the pledge or down payment of our inheritance:

> *Now He who establishes us with you in Christ and anointed us is God, who also sealed us and gave us the Spirit in our hearts as a pledge.* (2 Corinthians 1:21–22 NASB)

> *For all who are being led by the Spirit of God, these are sons of God. For you have not received a spirit of slavery leading to fear again, but you have received a spirit of adoption as sons by which we cry out, "Abba! Father!" The Spirit Himself testifies with our spirit that we are children of God, and if children, heirs also, heirs of God and fellow heirs with Christ, if indeed we suffer with Him so that we may also be glorified with Him.* (Romans 8:14–17 NASB)

Living under the Holy Spirit's influence, which means being led by Him, is a confirming sign that we are children of God. The adoption part of this story is quite amazing to me. In a very real sense, the presence of the indwelling Spirit in a believer is the proof the adoption was finalized. The Holy Spirit is the legal document declaring we belong to Him. The emphasis of the concept of adoption is that it was God's choice: He *chose* us.

Jesus, who lived among us on earth—empowered in all ways by the Holy Spirit—is now in heaven in His glorious resurrection body, sitting at the Father's right hand. (See, for example, Ephesians 1:20.) The Holy Spirit, who was first poured out on believers at Pentecost, remains on earth—dwelling in God's children and working among us. He is God on earth, immediately available to all who believe. This reality of Jesus's departure from earth and the Spirit's coming to us as *"another Helper"* (John 14:16) is to our complete advantage, just as it was for the apostles. Are you living in the fullness of this advantage? Do you want to learn more about how you can live in it each day? I welcome you into this adventure of having a continual, close relationship with the cherished Holy Spirit in which you are filled to overflowing with God's presence and power. I invite you to discover *The Holy Spirit: Who He Is and Why We Can't Live Without Him.*

PART ONE:

KNOWING THE UNKNOWABLE ONE

2

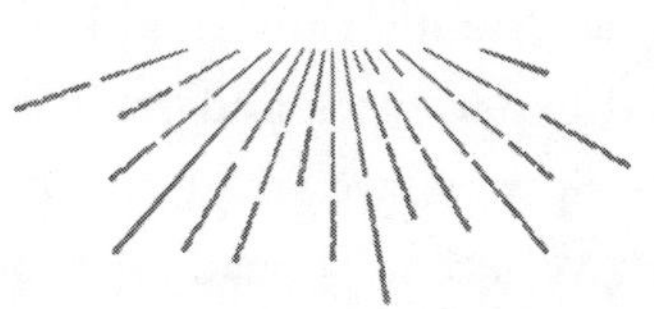

THE PERSON OF MYSTERY

In many ways, the Holy Spirit is a mystery to us. We understand more about Jesus, who lived on earth for thirty-three and a half years, than we do the Holy Spirit, who has been with the church on earth for almost two thousand years. This mystery seems even more ironic when we realize that most of what we know about the second person of the Trinity took place within the short, three and a half year period of Jesus's public ministry, compared with what we know about the third person of the Trinity from our two-thousand-year history with the Holy Spirit.

On a surface level, it is much easier for us to know more about Jesus than we know about the Holy Spirit because it is simpler to relate to someone who is in the flesh—human, like we are. Most of us don't yet recognize that, at our essence, we are spiritual beings who have a soul and a body. Because of this, we usually think and live from the natural world toward possible spiritual experiences and realities rather than from the spiritual world. In the Scriptures, we are given a clear description of Jesus, who revealed the Father. Whether by reading about Jesus's conversations, His working of miracles, or His profound teachings, finding a practical connection to Jesus is easier than relating to the Spirit of God, whom we can't see or even properly imagine, even with various descriptions of His manifestations in the Bible.

When God led the Israelites in the wilderness, His face was in the cloud that traveled with them. (See Exodus 13:21.) In the original languages in both the Old and New Testaments, "presence" is literally "face." It fits the Lord's command to us to "seek His face," to which the psalmist replied, "*Your face, Lord, I will seek*" (Psalm 27:8 NKJV). The face of God is our ultimate quest.

However, God wouldn't let the Israelites see any form of Himself because He knew them to be an idolatrous people who would create an image from what they saw. We are presented with a similar challenge of "seeing" God today. The Holy Spirit remains the face of God on the earth, yet He does not have a form we can see.

We don't have idols in our culture in the same way people did in the days of the Old and New Testaments (although, in Colossians 3:5, the apostle Paul calls greed idolatry, which certainly has application in our day). However, we do create *form*ulas and ideologies that attempt to replace our need for continuous dependency on the presence and voice of the Holy Spirit. We want what is tangible or concrete. As a result, we tend to gravitate toward principles for success over relationship with God when seeking personal transformation. Sometimes our lack of clarity reveals what we can be trusted with.

KNOWING WHAT IS BEYOND COMPREHENSION

Although the Holy Spirit is impossible to measure or quantify, this does not mean He is impossible to encounter. Many people envision the Holy Spirit as merely a force, an energy, or a "cosmic fog." But He is a divine person. As such, He understands you more fully than any human being does, and He can communicate with you in a way no other person could possibly do. In fact, having a personality, the Holy Spirit is relational by nature. Even more, He possesses everything necessary for entering into a fulfilling and adventurous relationship with each person on earth—at the same time. He always rejoices in having a heartfelt connection with those made in God's image.

The relational nature of the ever-present Holy Spirit and His loving heart toward us show us that *we must come to know Him.* Personally. The revelation of this nature is, in itself, an invitation to know Him. Understanding and accepting this invitation is essential for everyone because, in knowing Him, our purpose for being unfolds.

> *THE HOLY SPIRIT ALWAYS REJOICES IN HAVING A HEARTFELT CONNECTION WITH THOSE MADE IN GOD'S IMAGE.*

God made everything in creation perfect in beauty and design. Each part of it is an expression of some aspect of His nature. In Genesis 1, we read that at the end of each day of creation, God announced that the result of His work was *"good."* But of all that was made, both seen and unseen, only people were made in His image. And human beings are the only part of His creation that He declared to be *"very good."* (See Genesis 1:10, 12, 18, 21, 25, 31, various translations.) No other part of His creation carried such praise, promise, and purpose. We were designed for Him. Every other reason for being is inferior to that. God always had in mind both relationship and co-laboring with us. And we enter into that relationship and co-laboring through His Spirit.

In considering our relationship with our Creator, let's keep this very important biblical concept in mind: *we can know by experience what is beyond mental comprehension.* Those who develop a relationship with God through their natural understanding alone only end up with a god in their own image. It's supposed to be the other way around: we are created in the image of God; and, in Christ, we are being changed *"from glory to glory"* (2 Corinthians 3:18 NKJV, NASB) as we are exposed to God's manifest presence and yield to His glory, power, and will. Our thinking changes the more we understand and discover Him.

Our relationship with God has to originate, function, and grow through our spirit, or our heart. The heart is the place from which our faith flows. The Word says, *"With the heart one believes unto righteousness"* (Romans 10:10 NKJV). Not with the mind. The mind has to be trained to perceive correctly through a surrendered heart. Since the heart is the place of faith, it is only right that a relationship with the Holy Spirit comes from the heart. Great faith grows through our yielding, not our striving. That is how a relationship with God is nurtured: Surrendering. Yielding.

Only through surrender can we embark on and progress in this journey to know the One who is beyond knowing, from a natural standpoint. Having the mind of Christ is included in the inheritance of the believer. (See 1 Corinthians 2:16.) And under the influence of the Holy Spirit, our mind is the perfect partner and co-laborer with God. But when our mind isn't under the Spirit's influence, it opposes God. There is no neutral ground.

Because we were made in God's image, everything about us—spirit, soul, and body—is perfectly suited for a relationship with Him. Even our physical body, with its senses, was intended to help us experience and come to know Him. We were given this design so that we can feel and enjoy God's presence. Our senses can be trained to recognize what is from God, in contrast to what is not from God and is therefore wrong or lesser in value. (See Hebrews 5:14.)

When sin entered the human race through our disobedience toward God, our purpose of embarking on the eternal adventure of knowing Him was ambushed and destroyed. If it were not for God's grace, as evidenced in the death and resurrection of Christ, this purpose would have been lost forever. Anything that is demonic (that comes from Satan, God's enemy) is obviously at war with God. But it's important to recognize that whenever we settle for the inferior—which amounts to embracing values and decisions that lack eternal significance—that way of reasoning and living is at war with God too. Our relationship with the Holy Spirit is what clarifies God's purposes for us and enables us to live in the center of the mind of Christ.

Growing in our understanding of God has even greater importance when we realize that *insight is meant to lead to encounter.* Whatever knowledge about God we receive should lead to a deeper relationship with Him. The secret to real knowing is therefore the knowing of the heart.

I had an unusual (at least, for me) picture come to mind during a private time of worship a couple of hours before one of our Sunday church services was to begin. I was alone in my office, kneeling before the Lord, praying for that morning's gathering. As I knelt, I raised my hands before the Lord, with my face lifted heavenward, and declared the goodness and greatness of God. Then I experienced what I refer to as an internal vision. My eyes were closed, but the picture was very clear. I saw myself placing a crown on Jesus's head, and I knew this was a visible illustration of the effects of my praise for Him. It was a glorious moment. The crown was solid gold and had a mirrorlike finish. I can still see it whenever I recall this experience.

However, in the vision, when I removed my hands from the gold crown, I saw that my fingerprints had marred its beauty. I was so disappointed to have left such a blemish on the crown of glory that God deserved. I actually felt shame and disgust for my humanity, as it was the apparent cause of the blemish that had soiled my sacrifice of praise. But when I looked again, each fingerprint morphed into a costly gem. What I had despised was a treasure to God. That experience changed my life because I'd had a loathing for my humanity, which had been scarred by sin. In that moment,

I realized that, from His perspective, I was clean. Jesus's blood really has washed me clean from sin. The blood of Jesus doesn't do a halfway job or just enough to get us to heaven. His blood entirely restores us to Him as though we had never sinned. The Spirit of God within us manifests the nature of Jesus in and through us. I realized that sometimes what I despise, God treasures. The four Gospels exhibit this reality, multiplied a thousand times. This truth was not revealed to my mind but to my spirit, or my heart.

Ephesians 3 assures us we can know what is beyond knowing. In other words, our heart can take us where our head can't "fit." Paul's prayer for believers in this verse is quite challenging: that we would *"know the love of Christ which surpasses knowledge, that* [we] *may be filled up to all the fullness of God"* (Ephesians 3:19 NASB). Interestingly, once more, this petition points to an astounding invitation. We can experience that which surpasses knowledge, but it doesn't stop there. The conclusion of this incomprehensible statement is *"that you may be filled up to all the fullness of God."* Really? Filled with the fullness of God Himself? He fills the galaxies, holding every molecule in place through the power of His word. (See Colossians 1:17; Hebrews 1:3.) And this God has determined to *fill us* with His fullness? The surrender that leads to encounter paves the way for experiencing such extravagance.

The *Amplified* translation brings out the beauty of Ephesians 3:19 in a unique way:

> *And [that you may come] to know [practically,* ***through personal experience****] the love of Christ which far surpasses [mere] knowledge [without experience], that you may be filled up [throughout your being] to* ***all the fullness of God*** *[so that you may have the richest experience of God's presence in your lives,* ***completely filled and flooded with God Himself****].*

Could there be a greater promise than being *"completely filled and flooded with God Himself"*? I can't imagine what that could be! The concept of being filled with God is generally described with this phrase: "filled with the Holy Spirit." The Spirit is the One who fills us. In a very real sense, we were designed to contain and host the Holy Spirit Himself, a topic we will talk about further in a coming chapter.

As I described previously, the Bible is clear that the Holy Spirit is our down payment for eternal life. In other words, He has been given to us liberally, but, even so, there's more to come. I have no idea what that "more" looks like. But I find it fascinating to see that this is God's intention and plan for us. And Ephesians 3:19 underscores this truth.

INSIGHT IS MEANT TO LEAD TO ENCOUNTER. WHATEVER KNOWLEDGE WE RECEIVE FROM GOD SHOULD LEAD TO A DEEPER RELATIONSHIP WITH HIM.

THE MYSTERY AND UNITY OF THE GODHEAD

Helping people come to know the Holy Spirit, who is often a mystery to us, is one of my primary purposes for this book. Yet it's impossible for me to address this subject without also addressing the mystery of the Godhead. Few subjects in Scripture are more challenging to understand than the Trinity. But there are also few that are as beautiful.

Jesus taught us that the Father is perfectly seen and realized in the Son. But it's the Son of God who presents us with the most challenging and beautiful concept in Scripture: Jesus Christ is fully God yet fully man. R. T. Kendall says of Jesus that He was God as though He were not man at all, and He was man as though He were not God at all.[3] What a mystery—absolutely incomprehensible, wonderful, and inviting at the same time.

And then we bring the Holy Spirit into the picture, and it immensely compounds our difficulty in understanding who God is. My goal, when it

3. R. T. Kendall, "Imitating Christ 4," R. T. Kendall Ministries, https://rtkendallministries.com/imitating-christ-4.

comes to knowing God, is to not try to wrap my head fully around such thoughts, although I love to gain understanding. Instead, my goal is to expose my heart to the reality of who God is and what He is like. And then, through surrender, to let those realities shape my attitude, faith, and values, and forever alter my realization of His nature and works.

Jesus told us over and over again throughout the gospel of John that He came to reveal the Father. And in John 14:9, He said, "If you've seen Me, you've seen the Father." In Hebrews, Jesus is described as *"the exact representation of* [God's] *nature"* (Hebrews 1:3 NASB). It comes down to this: Jesus is the perfect example of what the Father is like; and, more importantly, He is the perfect manifestation of the Father. He is called *"the radiance of His glory"* (verse 3 NASB). To use a human illustration, Jesus emanates from the Father in a similar way to light shining forth from a lightbulb. The Father and the Son are distinct, uniquely separate from each other, and yet they are exactly the same.

The storytellers of the Gospels—Matthew, Mark, Luke, and John—let us in on the practical side of Jesus's earthly life. They include insights on the daily activities, reasonings, and dialogues of the eternal Son of God who became a man. These four men were allowed the privilege of recording in detail a representation of His values, thoughts, travels, interactions, and relationships, giving us a vivid picture of the Messiah—even though such an assignment is all but impossible. The Gospels describe the One who called Himself the Son of Man. And while each page reveals Jesus, ultimately, it also reveals the Father, because revealing the Father was Jesus's primary assignment.

When Jesus introduced the fact that the Holy Spirit would be sent, He stated, *"And I will pray the Father, and He will give you another Helper, that He may abide with you forever..., for He dwells with you and will be in you"* (John 14:16–17 NKJV). The Holy Spirit was sent to us as an answer to the prayers of Jesus Christ, the eternal Son of God. Jesus could have asked for anything and received it, but He chose this one thing: the Holy Spirit, who had been with the disciples but would now take up residence in them, making them His temple. Jesus prayed this prayer because it was the best thing He could have prayed. As I wrote in chapter 1, for this reason, Jesus told His disciples, in effect, "It is better that I go." (See John 16:7.) The Holy Spirit *in* them was better than Jesus *with* them.

Many people point out that the Holy Spirit does not *"speak on His own authority"* (John 16:13). For some reason, this has become an excuse for some to give Him a mere courteous mention, and even then only as an aspect of theological doctrine, while ignoring Him entirely in purpose, practice, and relationship in daily life. What does it mean that the Holy Spirit does not speak on His own authority? It means that He points us to Jesus on behalf of the Father. That is how the Spirit reveals Himself to us. He reveals Himself by what He does: *He is the One who honors the Father and Jesus. The One who directs us in worship to Them.* The practice of giving honor is seen among the members of the Godhead. But the role of the Holy Spirit is unique in that He lives in us and is now to be the primary influence on how we live *for the glory of God.*

One might ask why all this discussion about the Trinity is important to consider at the beginning of a book devoted to our understanding of the Holy Spirit. It is because Jesus exactly represents and reveals the Father, and it's the Holy Spirit who exactly represents and reveals the Son. So, when we see revelation of the nature of God the Father or God the Son, we are seeing things that are ultimately discovered and more fully understood through the Holy Spirit, who is God with us. While the members of the Trinity are distinct, They are three unique expressions of the same presence, heart, and nature. Thus, *interaction with the Holy Spirit is the way to discover both the wonder and the power of the Father and the Son.*

Throughout this book, I will interchange talking about the Holy Spirit with the Father and the Son, using the latter to illustrate the specifics of the Holy Spirit's nature.

VALUING MYSTERY

Even though our knowledge and understanding of God is always to be increasing, we can never fully comprehend Him. We will keep learning more about Him throughout eternity. Here's the very unusual reality we live in: while our knowledge of God increases, the mystery of Him increases all the more. It is vital for us to live in this tension in order to enter into all that He has purposed for us in this life.

Valuing the quality of mystery will help us keep the fear of the Lord intact in our lives, while making this relational journey with Him a continual adventure. If I only obey what I understand, I have reduced God to my size. I have, as we talked about earlier, fashioned a god in my own image. Mystery surrounding God is essential, if for no other reason than to prompt us to prove we trust Him even though we can't understand everything about Him. While understanding more about God brings us awe and celebration, increased mystery about Him gives us the opportunity to trust Him in our divine partnership with Him. Mysteries are wonderful opportunities to exercise the divine perceptions of the heart.

THE ESSENCE OF KINGDOM REASONING

Although the Holy Spirit is mysterious by nature because He is Spirit, we must realize that since He is God, He is also the essence of practicality and reasonableness. But be forewarned: His is the reasoning of another world, one much superior to ours in every way. A comprehension of such reasoning is usually found where there is a willing heart, not just a curious mind. The Roman centurion whose story is found in Matthew 8:5–13 wonderfully illustrates this truth. He was outside of the house of Israel and had no obvious spiritual training, but his understanding of spiritual authority stunned even the Master Himself, Jesus. My point is this: if a Roman centurion can get it, so can we. It is within our reach. Surrendering to God, with the willingness to obey whatever He says, is the key.

The Spirit longs to introduce us to such reasonings. We understand them through the mind of Christ that we've inherited. I receive revelation from the Spirit, often with such depth that it is difficult to fully comprehend it, but I am willing to live with that mystery. (Please note that such revelation is not *in place of* the revelation of Scripture.) In fact, a willingness to trust God with what I don't understand often precedes increased understanding. Some people say, "We don't need God to speak to us because we have the Bible." This is one of the more popular excuses people use to avoid learning to hear the voice of God. But, in Christ, we have been given the spiritual capacity to hear God's voice. Jesus Himself said, *"My sheep hear My voice"* (John 10:27 NKJV, NASB). The ability to hear Him comes in our *yes* to follow Him. Many believers avoid His voice because, in ignorance, they fear what they can't explain. These believers quarantine themselves from other parts of the body of Christ that have something to offer them to make their lives better: revelation about the Holy Spirit and the way He works. All of us are to be strengthened by what each member of the body provides. It is for the purpose of helping us in our daily life of walking with, and depending on, the Holy Spirit.

Hearing from the Holy Spirit actually drives me *to* the Scriptures. Not only does reading the Scriptures help me to verify whether what I have sensed is biblically correct, but the Spirit's voice also endears me to the Word of God, which brings life with every page. My Bible is Jesus in print. He is the Word of God. The promises, the warnings, the mysteries—all of it represents Him. To love Him but not love His Word is a contradiction. It's my relationship with the Spirit of Christ that draws me into the Word of God over and over again. The time I spend reading and studying Scripture is part of my journey with the Holy Spirit.

The Holy Spirit takes us *"from glory to glory"* (2 Corinthians 3:18 NKJV, NASB). And we are to anticipate receiving this "more" because this is His heart for us: "[Jesus] *said, 'To you it has been granted to know the mysteries of the kingdom of God'"* (Luke 8:10 NASB). It is the Holy Spirit who is the Revealer of truth to us all: *"But when He, the Spirit of truth, comes, He will guide you into all the truth; for He will not speak on His own initiative, but whatever He hears, He will speak; and He will disclose to you what is to come"* (John 16:13 NASB).

It's easier for some people to create a theological reason for their resistance to hearing directly from God than it is to own up to their responsibility to discover His voice in this relational journey. We have an invitation to learn to hear God through fellowship with the Holy Spirit. Anyone who thinks they can grasp the depth of the Word of God, with its transformational power, without the inspiration of the

Holy Spirit is delusional! The Spirit is the One who leads us into all truth. (See John 16:13.) In later chapters, we will talk more about how to hear God's voice.

We must remember that God has already purposed to reveal His secrets to His people. This is not an idea made up by Pentecostals and charismatics. It is found in the early writings of Scripture: *"The secret things belong to the* L*ORD our God, but the things which are revealed belong to us and to our children forever, that we may do all the words of this law"* (Deuteronomy 29:29 NKJV). Thus, God has always intended to show His secrets to His people, who would then steward them as an inheritance to give to subsequent generations. Such proper stewardship attracts the voice of the Lord to build upon that generation's understanding with deeper and more meaningful truths. This is why the writer of Hebrews said, *"Not laying again a foundation..."* (Hebrews 6:1 NASB). There's more for us in Christ. It's time for us to go where the truths we have discovered were always intended to take us. And, from there, to build upon what we already understand.

> ***MY RELATIONSHIP WITH THE SPIRIT OF CHRIST DRAWS ME INTO THE WORD OF GOD OVER AND OVER AGAIN. THE TIME I SPEND READING AND STUDYING SCRIPTURE IS PART OF MY JOURNEY WITH THE HOLY SPIRIT.***

A REALM OF FREEDOM

In the mystery of the Godhead, God the Father is upon His throne in heaven, the Son of God is seated at His right hand, and the Holy Spirit is God on earth, living in His eternal dwelling place, His temple: God's people. As expressed earlier, the Spirit is the One who enables us to succeed in all the Father has assigned us to be and do. As we come to know this "Person of Mystery," we will enter into a deeper relationship with Him.

What I have learned from years of experience and studying the Scriptures is that the Holy Spirit is expert at listening without reacting, kind in His responses, genuine—never artificial—and honest in a way that serves us well while also setting us free from inferior things in our lives without bringing us shame. He continues to welcome us even when we fall short, when we go to Him in fear, anger, resentment, or unbelief. However, He also has no tolerance for sin, which is anything that is contrary to His holy and loving nature. He has no intention of giving us an "audience with the King" yet allowing us to leave the same way we entered. Knowing Him changes us. Completely. Perhaps I should put it this way: under such circumstances, if we leave our time of prayer in the same manner in which we came to it, we weren't praying—we were complaining.

The Holy Spirit always works to bring us into His realm of freedom. In fact, it can be said that the amount of influence He has in a person's life is measured by the freedom in which they live. The Spirit manifests the Prince of Peace. He is always present, never distracted, and never too busy for us. He values faith more than we realize because, as God, He is the most trustworthy one in existence. Our faith in Him is powerful only because of His perfect trustworthiness. When we consider God's nature of complete faithfulness, faith is our only reasonable response.

3

BECOMING A RESTING PLACE

In the New Testament, the Holy Spirit takes center stage—nothing happens without Him. He is the Spirit of Christ. He raises Jesus from the dead, enables believers to be like Jesus in character and in power, and demonstrates the atmosphere of heaven here on earth. While it is true that He does not speak about Himself, both Jesus and the Father speak about Him often. Once again, the Trinity does a beautiful dance in which each honors the other in perfect harmony, revealing one heart, one mind, and one will.

On the other hand, the Old Testament provides some of the richest *insights* into the Holy Spirit. Scripture's revelation about the Holy Spirit under the old covenant is enlightening, as those insights set the stage for everything revealed about Him in the New Testament. Comparing the process of biblical revelation to a flowering plant, the New Testament is the blossom, but the Old Testament is the root system. The root system is what holds the flower in place, provides nutrients to the whole plant, and even sustains it. The Spirit's nature and heart become obvious in the Old Testament's graphic illustrations of His presence and works.

NOAH'S MISSION

For example, the presence of the Holy Spirit is manifested and symbolized in unique forms in the book of Genesis. In some ways, my favorite illustration from that book is connected to the great man Noah. Noah was commanded to build an ark, a very large boat that would sustain the lives of both human beings and animals during the great flood that was to come upon the earth. Noah's obedience to build the ark and find refuge in it with his family was followed by forty days and nights of rain, until the whole earth was flooded. (See Genesis 6–7.)

Noah waited inside the ark until he knew it was time to obey the next steps in God's plan. He knew it was the right time by "testing the waters":

> *He also sent out from himself a dove, to see if the waters had receded from the face of the ground. But the dove found no resting place for the sole of her foot, and she* ***returned into the ark to him,*** *for the waters were on the face of the whole earth. So he put out his hand and took her, and* ***drew her into the ark to himself.*** *And he waited yet another seven days, and again* ***he sent the dove out from the ark.*** *Then* ***the dove came to him in the evening, and behold, a freshly plucked olive leaf was in her mouth;*** *and Noah knew that the waters had receded from the earth. So* ***he waited yet another seven days and sent out the dove, which did not return again to him anymore.***
>
> (Genesis 8:8–12 NKJV)

In this beautiful story, Noah used a dove to find out if the floodwaters had receded enough that he and his family could leave the boat and start life on land again. When the dove found no resting place, she returned to the ark. Noah seemed to have a personal connection with this dove because the emphasis is on the fact that he *"drew her into the ark to himself."* He waited seven days and then tried again. This time, the dove returned after having been gone for a good part of the day. When she came back, she had an olive leaf in her mouth. That, of course, was a sign that the waters were receding, vegetation was growing again, and it wouldn't be long before Noah and his family could leave the boat. Noah finally released the dove after another seven days of waiting. This time, she did not return again.

The international symbol of peace is an olive branch in the mouth of a dove. This symbol is no doubt taken from this biblical story, which provides us with a profound symbol of peace for the church as well. The dove represents the peace and restoration that the Holy Spirit brings us through Christ.

Because of his obedience, Noah preserved the lives of his family members from the destructive force of the flood that covered the earth. He, his wife, his sons, and his sons' spouses were all saved, as were the lives of those in the animal kingdom that had been brought on board for preservation. Two, male and female, of each unclean animal, seven pairs of each clean animal, and seven pairs of birds were brought onto the ark. (See Genesis 7:2–3.) This would have made it possible for Noah to give a sacrifice of one clean animal of each species and still have three pairs left for breeding. Both mankind and the animal kingdom were to repopulate the earth.

In a sense, the earth was being reborn. The evil of the days previous to the flood had reached a maximum level and had to be destroyed. Noah and his children would now have a chance to start over. It was a day of new beginnings.

THE DOVE REPRESENTS THE PEACE AND RESTORATION THAT THE HOLY SPIRIT BRINGS US THROUGH CHRIST.

JESUS'S MISSION

Notably, when a person is born again, he or she becomes a new creation and is given a brand-new start. "*Therefore, if anyone is in Christ, he is a new creation; old things have passed away; behold, all things have become new*" (2 Corinthians 5:17 NKJV). From the time of the creation of humanity to the time of Christ, there had never been anything newly created—no *new* creation. (Noah was given the opportunity of a new beginning but not of becoming a new creation.) After the sacrificial death and resurrection of Jesus, human beings had the opportunity to be born again by the Spirit of God—the One who raised Christ from the dead. Whenever someone is born again, that person actually becomes something that has never existed before!

Peter describes the phenomenon in this way:

> *But* ***you are a chosen generation, a royal priesthood, a holy nation, His own special people****, that you may proclaim the praises of Him who called you out of darkness into His marvelous light; who once were not a people but* ***are now the people of God****, who had not obtained mercy but* ***now have obtained mercy****.* (1 Peter 2:9–10 NKJV)

The descriptors of this new creation found in the above passage are simply beautiful. The purpose is equally wonderful: that we may proclaim God's praises!

Peter was "in the room" when this story of the new creation began to unfold. He had witnessed Jesus's crucifixion. (See Luke 23:49.) He was aware of where Jesus's body had been placed in the tomb. (See, for example, Luke 23:55.) He had even seen the empty tomb on the morning of the resurrection:

> *Then Simon Peter came, following him* [John]*, and went into the tomb; and he saw the linen cloths lying there, and the handkerchief that had been around His head, not lying with the linen cloths, but folded together in a place by itself. Then the other disciple, who came to the tomb first, went in also; and he saw and believed. For* ***as yet they did***

not know the Scripture, that He must rise again from the dead.
(John 20:6–9 NKJV)

Even though the tomb was empty, Peter and John had no idea at first what that meant for them. Yet this was to become their day of new beginnings. This was to become the day when they discovered the world was completely different from what it had been only a few days earlier. The flood of God's grace had destroyed the powers of darkness that had been killing, stealing, and destroying the lives of humanity ever since Noah was given a clean start. (See John 10:10.) The Holy Spirit living in the disciples would make it possible for them to demonstrate the superior nature of God's kingdom and see it become manifest in practical ways in the lives of broken people.

THE ROOM BEFORE THE UPPER ROOM

Immediately after Jesus was crucified, fear gripped the remaining eleven disciples so much that they went into hiding. Not even the fact that Peter and John had seen the empty tomb helped to calm the nerves of the terrified group following this traumatic experience. They had seen the brutal death of their Master. Their identity was widely known to people, so much so that a servant girl could tell that Peter was a follower of Jesus. (See, for example, Mark 14:66–72.) They were certain they would be killed next, as that is the way the Roman government worked.

The disciples hid in a room in an unnamed location. Upper or lower level, no one knows. All we know for sure is that the darkest room ever, which was being controlled by fear and panic—the Eleven having just witnessed the most gruesome death of all time—was about to become the room where everything changed. It changed because Jesus came, walking into that room where all doors had been shut for the disciples' safety.

Then, the same day at evening, being the first day of the week, when the ***doors were shut*** *where the disciples were assembled,* ***for fear*** *of the Jews,* ***Jesus came*** *and stood in the midst, and said to them,* ***"Peace be with you."*** *When He had said this, He showed them His hands and*

> *His side. Then the disciples were glad when they saw the Lord. So Jesus said to them again, "**Peace to you!** As the Father has sent Me, I also send you." And when He had said this, He breathed on them, and said to them, "**Receive the Holy Spirit**. If you forgive the sins of any, they are forgiven them; if you retain the sins of any, they are retained."*
>
> (John 20:19–23 NKJV)

I'm sure that when Jesus suddenly arrived, it didn't help the disciples with their fear issues. They were already terrified. Notice they didn't immediately recognize Him, which had to have added to the terror of the moment. Jesus had to show them the scars from the wounds on His hands and side for them to know who He was. The phenomenon of Jesus's appearance being different from what it was when they knew Him in His earthly form before His death is seen a number of times throughout the post-resurrection story. And Jesus continues to manifest Himself to us in various ways to this day. But when He does manifest, it is always in a way consistent with Scripture and never in violation of the Holy Spirit's nature and ways. To this point, we must study the Word of God and become tenderly familiar with and connected to the Spirit of God, who always reveals the Father's heart.

A PLACE TO LAND

Before Jesus revealed His identity to the disciples, He told them, *"Peace be with you"* (John 20:19). Imagine with me this moment when Jesus released peace. I think it was much like Noah's releasing of the dove from the ark the first time, when there was nowhere for the dove to land. In Noah's case, the reason was that the floodwaters had not yet receded from the earth. In Jesus's case, the floodwaters of fear had not yet receded from the hearts and minds of the disciples, even though the resurrected One—the One who had defeated death, sin, and all the powers of darkness—was now in the room. If they had recognized the divine moment they were in, they would not have feared anything!

The dove (peace) had not found anywhere to land that was safe. But once Jesus revealed who He was by showing the disciples the scars of

His suffering, the flood of fear within them diminished, and the dove now had a place to settle. The Scriptures say, *"Then the disciples were glad when they saw the Lord"* (verse 20). It's quite obvious that they *weren't* glad the first time around! Jesus released the dove again when He said, *"Peace to you!"* (verse 21). This time, He followed the pronouncement of peace with the gift that was to make Noah's day of new beginnings pale in comparison. He breathed on them and said, *"Receive the Holy Spirit"* (verse 22).

Noah received a clean start to a new day, but the disciples *became* the new day: a new creation. As we read earlier, Peter described believers in Jesus as *"a chosen generation, a royal priesthood, a holy nation, His own special people"* (1 Peter 2:9). The same Holy Spirit who hovered over the waters on the day of creation and brought forth all things new (see Genesis 1:2) was now residing in God's people. The Spirit of the resurrected Christ took up residence in them. His blood-bought ones had become the temple of the living God. The dove found not only a safe place to land, but also a place that would honor Him and give Him the rightful position of influence in and through their lives. *Being led by the Spirit* was no longer a pipe dream. It was a reality freely given to all who confessed Jesus as Lord.

One of the parts of this story of the new creation that is both the most challenging and the most inviting to me is Jesus's comment, *"As the Father has sent me, I also send you"* (John 20:21). What was Jesus sent to do? Reveal the Father and release the Holy Spirit. What are we assigned to do? Reveal the Father and release the Holy Spirit.

> ***BEING LED BY THE SPIRIT WAS NO LONGER A PIPE DREAM. IT WAS A REALITY FREELY GIVEN TO ALL WHO CONFESSED JESUS AS LORD.***

IMPARTING PEACE

It is my conviction that the disciples hadn't understood what Jesus meant earlier in their journey together when He instructed them to let their peace rest upon a house:

> *But whatever house you enter, first say, "**Peace to this house.**" And if a son of peace is there, your peace will rest on it; if not, **it will return to you.** And remain in the same house, eating and drinking such things as they give, for the laborer is worthy of his wages. Do not go from house to house. Whatever city you enter, and they receive you, eat such things as are set before you. And **heal the sick there,** and say to them, "**The kingdom of God has come near to you.**"* (Luke 10:5–9 NKJV)

If the disciples had not previously understood what Jesus had instructed them to do, it's reasonable to expect that their understanding skyrocketed following their experience with Him walking through the wall into their presence and releasing peace over them in their time of great fear. In Luke 10, as if He had been prophesying about them, Jesus had said that if a *"son of peace"* was not in the house, the peace would return. I believe that is exactly what happened to Jesus. The dove returned to Him. So He tried again. Most of us are alive because God is the God of second chances.

Romans 14:17 (NKJV) says, *"**For the kingdom of God** is not eating and drinking, but righteousness and peace and joy **in the Holy Spirit.**"* The kingdom of God is in the realm of the Holy Spirit. And there is no more sickness in the realm of the Holy Spirit than there would be in heaven itself, for the Holy Spirit demonstrates the lordship of Jesus over every enemy of mankind. The passage from Luke 10 (NKJV) carries all of these elements: *"peace to this house"* (verse 5), *"heal the sick there"* (verse 9), and *"the kingdom of God has come near to you"* (verse 9).

Note that the three terms Paul used to summarize the nature of God's kingdom are *righteousness, peace,* and *joy.*

Righteousness reveals God's perfect nature as seen in purity, beauty, power, and glory. It is beyond being sinless. It is the essence of His goodness, which has no compromise, distraction, dilution, or divided interests.

Another word for this in our world is *excellence*. As such, it is separate from everything inferior. In the realm of God's dominion, there is nothing defiled or less than perfect.

Peace is not just the *absence* of something, such as the absence of noise, conflict, or war. It is the *presence* of Someone. More specifically, it is the prevailing presence of the Spirit of God, who appropriately reveals the Prince of Peace, Jesus Christ, in a given location and/or situation. Peace conquers everything contrary to itself and brings it under the glorious rule and influence of this ruling One.

Joy is absolute pure delight, pleasure, and perfect ecstasy. In a very real sense, joy is the essence of the nature of God, manifested in the garden of Eden, experienced by Adam and Eve. As surely as we were created for fellowship with God, we were designed for joy. Psalm 16:11 (NKJV) says, *"In Your presence is fullness of joy; at Your right hand are pleasures forevermore."* Notice the connection between the presence of God and the experience of joy for us as individuals. The words *"fullness"* and *"pleasures"* are descriptors of our relationship with God. These two words reveal the nature of the Holy Spirit's influence in a believer's life. And it is *fullness* of joy, which implies "nothing lacking." This concept is also mentioned in John 16:24, which expresses that having our desires fulfilled through answered prayers gives us access to that same measure of joy.

From their experience of Jesus appearing in their midst and imparting peace, the disciples were to learn that we can and must release the presence of the dove, the Spirit of peace, over homes and businesses that we enter. Coming to recognize His presence upon us is a critical part of our maturing process. Because Jesus lived with an awareness of *the dove on His shoulder*, He knew when power left His body and healed the woman who had pressed through the crowd to touch the hem of His garment. (See Luke 8:43–48.) In a similar way, as we become familiar with the Spirit's presence, we can become more aware when we have entered a place where people of peace are present because the dove/peace "rests" and doesn't return to us, as Noah illustrated and Jesus described to His disciples.

After the resurrection of Christ, the new day was not marked by an empty earth, about to be repopulated by man and beast. This time, it was—and is—marked by the transformation of individuals from the inside out. That is the best kind of *new day.* The clean canvas was not an earth that was empty of life. The clean canvas was and is the untouched territory called the human heart, ready to be transformed by God's Spirit into the image of Jesus.

4

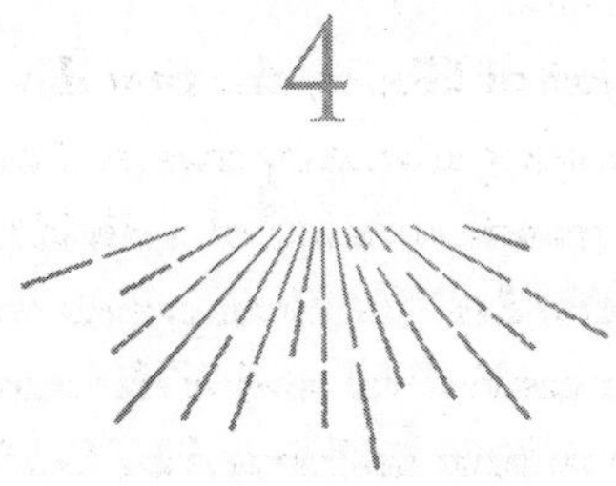

BEING TRANSFORMED INTO THE IMAGE OF JESUS

Jesus introduced His disciples to the Spirit of God, who would introduce them further to their heavenly Father, so they could live the corresponding lifestyle they had once observed only in Jesus. This Spirit would lead them as He had led Jesus and continually connect them to Abba Father; He would witness to their spirits that they had been adopted by God and were now joint heirs with Jesus.

As we read in chapter 1 of this book, the Holy Spirit living within us is the seal of our adoption:

> *For as many as are led by the Spirit of God, these are sons of God. For you did not receive the spirit of bondage again to fear, but you received the Spirit of adoption* ***by whom we cry out, "Abba, Father."*** *The Spirit Himself bears witness with our spirit that we are children of God, and if children, then heirs—heirs of God and joint heirs with Christ, if indeed we suffer with Him, that we may also be glorified together.* (Romans 8:14–17 NKJV)

One of the things I enjoy immensely is watching adoption stories on YouTube. They bring me to tears over and over again. The stories often center on a child holding a sign that says something like, "After months of being in foster care and living in five different foster homes, I AM BEING ADOPTED!" The joy on these children's faces—absolute perfection—is worth every sacrifice their adopted families make for such a change in their homes and lifestyles. Another story that moves me just as deeply is when a stepdad will give a special Christmas gift to his stepchild. The love in the home is already obvious. But when that young boy or girl, often in their teenage years, opens the gift and reads of the stepdad's desire to adopt them and give them his name, oh my, tears flow. The joy becomes palpable to me, even though I am watching the scenario unfold on a computer screen. Perhaps the situation that wrecks me the most is when a young girl gives her stepdad a letter for Christmas that says, "Will you adopt me?" I'm a mess every time I see something like that. To be honest, I am weeping even now as I write this.

Multiply the stories I've just told by a thousand, and you'll begin to understand the word used to describe our adoption by God. It says we received the Holy Spirit *"by whom we cry out, 'Abba Father.'"* One of the meanings of the Greek word translated as *"cry out"* is "to scream."[4] And the passage says *"by whom,"* implying that the Holy Spirit is the source of the cry or outburst, affirming our identity by introducing us to our

---

4. *Strong's*, G2896, Blue Letter Bible Lexicon, https://www.blueletterbible.org/lexicon/g2896/kjv/tr/0-1/.

Father. This type of cry would not fit into many people's definition of doing things in the church *"decently and in order"* (1 Corinthians 14:40 NKJV) because it is raw, real, and extreme. But it is from the Holy Spirit, and it is part of our life with this Father! This is a stunning picture of the role of the Holy Spirit: to introduce us to, and strengthen our identity with, the Father.

Jesus's primary role on earth was to reveal the Father. But it wasn't until He released the Holy Spirit that His assignment was complete, for only in the indwelling of the Holy Spirit do we find out who we are because of who our Father is. This is a relational revelation in that we can now personally know the Father, the One so often celebrated by Jesus.

> ***JESUS'S PRIMARY ROLE ON EARTH WAS TO REVEAL THE FATHER. BUT IT WASN'T UNTIL HE RELEASED THE HOLY SPIRIT THAT HIS ASSIGNMENT WAS COMPLETE.***

GIVING BIRTH

Just as Jesus revealed the Father, we, too, are now called to reveal Him to others. The Holy Spirit demonstrates the heart of the Father to and through us as He transforms us into the image of Jesus, our Elder Brother. This transformation process is exciting, but it can be messy at times!

I was in the room for all three of my children's births. My wife Beni and I were grateful that the births did not involve any medical emergencies or other frightening complications that so many parents have to endure. But to the ignorant, of which I was one, the process of giving birth did not look *decent and in order*. It was messy. Really messy. And yet the doctors and nurses exhibited great peace and even joy in both the process and the outcome. What a wonderful day it was, each time, because my wife and I received the most amazing gifts ever: three wonderful children. But what seemed chaotic from the viewpoint of the ignorant was actually in order and quite beautiful to those *in the know*. I had to receive confidence from the peace of the experts. Their confidence became my own.

Jesus likened our conversion to a birth, using the words *"born again"* (John 3:3, 7, various translations). While I don't like chaos and disorder, I have to remember whose definition of order I am to stand by when it comes to spiritual matters. It is the Holy Spirit who inspires *"groanings which cannot be uttered"* (Romans 8:26 NKJV) and cries of *"Abba, Father"* (Romans 8:15, various translations). His definition stands.

Perhaps the one "church service" of all time that the Holy Spirit was fully in charge of was the day of Pentecost. No one knew enough then to mess it up!

> *Now there were Jews living in Jerusalem, devout men from every nation under heaven. And when this sound occurred, the crowd came together, and were* ***bewildered****.... They were* ***amazed*** *and* ***astonished****.... And they all continued in* ***amazement*** *and* ***great perplexity****, saying to one another, "What does this mean?" But others were* ***mocking*** *and saying, "They are full of sweet wine."* (Acts 2:5–7, 12–13 NASB)

When the Holy Spirit was fully in charge, *bewilderment, amazement, astonishment, great perplexity,* and *mocking* were the fruits seen in the crowd that was present. Many people make the mistake of defining the will of God by what makes them comfortable. Yes, He is the Comforter. But He often makes us uncomfortable first so that we can stretch and grow. His constant attention to change challenges us not to live in a counterfeit comfort but to truly live with absolute trust in the One who knows what He is doing and where we are going.

Likewise, it is far too easy for us to define the nature of God by what we like about ourselves. We often protect what is a dysfunctional attitude or behavior in contrast to the life modeled by Jesus; we give it a virtuous name, by which we give it permission to stay. For example, if we like the fact that we are hard to impress, resistant to new ideas, or skeptical of the supernatural, we often credit God with having these traits. People who are overly cautious are usually called "wise." But they rarely move any mountains. Such dysfunctions are costly in the long run.

So many times, when I have talked about the supernatural aspects of our faith, people have come to me saying they are more intellectual in nature and don't relate to the supernatural or need it in their lives. But can we call a perspective *intelligent* if it is not anchored in the mind of Christ? The miraculous comes from Christ's intellect. A mindset that dismisses the supernatural is nothing but a reflection of brokenness. *Brokenness* may seem like a strange way to describe it, as caution and skepticism about spiritual matters are often the traits most celebrated by our peers, both within and outside of the church. But they are a primary target of the Lord as He works to transform our way of thinking and our way of seeing to a kingdom perspective. I'm so thankful for His kindnesses toward me when He often has to pull me out of a wrong way of thinking. Our aligning with the mind of Christ will help us to remain as a welcome resting place for the Holy Spirit and to stay open to the ways in which He is working in us.

> ***THE HOLY SPIRIT DEMONSTRATES THE HEART OF THE FATHER TO AND THROUGH US AS HE TRANSFORMS US INTO THE IMAGE OF JESUS, OUR ELDER BROTHER.***

THE MIRROR OF MIRRORS

We have seen that the Holy Spirit is exactly like Jesus; He is referred to as "*another Helper*" in John 14:16 (NASB, NKJV). And we know that Jesus is exactly like the Father. Remember that Jesus told His disciples that if they had seen Him, they had seen the Father. (See John 14:9.) The writer of Hebrews wonderfully expresses this reality:

> *He is the radiance of His glory and* ***the exact representation of His nature****, and upholds all things by the word of His power. When He had made purification of sins, He sat down at the right hand of the Majesty on high.* (Hebrews 1:3 NASB)

The Holy Spirit is continually making us like Jesus, who is seated at the right hand of the Father in heaven. One of the most mind-boggling scriptural statements in this regard is found in the apostle Paul's second epistle to the church at Corinth:

> *But if the ministry of death, written and engraved on stones, was glorious, so that the children of Israel could not look steadily at the face of Moses because of the glory of his countenance, which glory was passing away,* ***how will the ministry of the Spirit not be more glorious?...*** *For if what is passing away was glorious, what remains is much more glorious.... For until this day the same veil remains unlifted in the reading of the Old Testament, because the veil is taken away in Christ. But even to this day, when Moses is read, a veil lies on their heart. Nevertheless when one turns to the Lord, the veil is taken away. Now the Lord is the Spirit; and* ***where the Spirit of the Lord is, there is liberty****. But we all, with unveiled face,* ***beholding as in a mirror the glory of the Lord, are being transformed into the same image from glory to glory, just as by the Spirit of the Lord.***
> (2 Corinthians 3:7–8, 11, 14–18 NKJV)

Do you see what this passage is indicating—that we're beholding the glory of the Lord but then discovering we're looking in a mirror? In that mirror, we are seeing the work of the Holy Spirit, who is transforming us "*from glory to glory*" into the image of the glorified Son of God.

Brian Simmons of *The Passion Translation* puts it brilliantly:

Now the "Lord" I'm referring to is the Holy Spirit, and wherever he is Lord, there is freedom.... We are being transfigured into his very image as we move from one brighter level of glory to another. And this glorious transfiguration comes from the Lord, who is the Spirit.

(2 Corinthians 3:17–18)

DESIGNED FOR GLORY

"For all have sinned and fall short of the glory of God" (Romans 3:23, various translations). We were designed to live in the glory of God. Of course, sin caused us to fall short of God's original intent for us. But Jesus's blood restored us to His original design by destroying the power and record of sin. The Holy Spirit brings the glory of the perfect Son of God into the lives of born-again believers, transforming each of us into the image of Jesus, who is now glorified in heaven.

Before there was sin, there was an answer to it because Jesus was crucified before sin entered the world. The Scriptures state, *"All who dwell on the earth will worship him* [the beast], *whose names have not been written in the Book of Life of* ***the Lamb slain from the foundation of the world"*** (Revelation 13:8 NKJV). This great mystery reveals the heart of God from eternity past for those who would be made in His image. Nothing—not the devil, not sin, not even our rebellion—can destroy God's plan of having people live in His glory without blemish. This seamless connection is possible only because of the blood of the spotless Lamb of God and the sanctifying work of the Holy Spirit, described in this verse: *"Elect according to the foreknowledge of God the Father, in* ***sanctification of the Spirit,*** *for obedience and* ***sprinkling of the blood of Jesus Christ:*** *Grace to you and peace be multiplied"* (1 Peter 1:2 NKJV). We are not marginally qualified to live in God's glory. We are *completely* qualified to live in the glory because of the effectiveness of the blood of Jesus.

Therefore, the Holy Spirit makes it possible for us to behold God's glory as though we were looking in a mirror, seeing what He has done in our lives. And this overwhelming miracle of grace happens because we always become like the one we worship. We become like the one we behold.

Jesus is exactly like the Father. The Holy Spirit is exactly like Jesus. And we are becoming exactly like the glorified Son of God through the working of the Spirit, who leads us to our Father.

5

MADE TO HOST

We have seen that the journey of humanity's connection with the Holy Spirit started at the beginning of time, in the garden of Eden. Heaven and earth merged beautifully there, allowing the first man and woman to experience their purpose as those made in God's image: *joy*. The Hebrew word *eden* means "delight," luxury," or "pleasure."[5] I'm amazed at how often we miss this meaning, which is meant to draw our attention to God's original purpose for us. He is a good, good Father who created us for His pleasure and ours.

5. Ernest Klein, *A Comprehensive Etymological Dictionary of the Hebrew Language for Readers of English*, 1st ed. (Carta Jerusalem, 1987), Sefaria, https://www.sefaria.org/Klein_Dictionary%2C_%D7%A2%D6%B5%D6%BD%D7%93%D6%B6%D7%9F_%E1%B4%B5?lang=bi.

The garden of Eden is where God regularly met and fellowshipped with Adam. There is no biblical record of how long this blissful state of fellowship went on before Eve was made. Nor does the Bible mention how long it was after the creation of Eve, who enjoyed the same fellowship with God, that she and Adam disobeyed the Lord and ate of the forbidden fruit. It could easily have been many years.

The Holy Spirit most assuredly filled this wonderful paradise, for it would not have been paradise without Him. The Holy Spirit is the One who demonstrates the rule of God's kingship. He contains the essence of God's kingdom (the King's domain) within His person. The kingdom is revealed and contained in the Spirit's manifest presence. To come to know Him is to come to know and experience the reality of God's kingdom. And to explore the reality of the kingdom of God is to engage in the journey of a lifetime in a relationship with the Holy Spirit.

The garden of Eden was thus the ultimate earthly paradise, filled with the presence of almighty God. As I described earlier, the air was permeated with righteousness, peace, and joy, which are among the expressions of His blissful rule. Eden contained the perfect beauty of God's creation; the ecstatic delight found in Adam and Eve, who were living without sin and shame; and the eternal wonder of this everlasting Father, who chose to reveal Himself to, in, and through human beings. This garden of pleasure and perfection was to illustrate yet another aspect of God's wonder, beauty, and design that could not be revealed as clearly through any other part of His creation, as this was the only part that we know of that was designed with the priority of pleasure in mind.

This garden of perfect bliss was *other* than heaven, but it was not contrary or inferior to heaven (although it became inferior because of sin). Eden was the ultimate earthly paradise because the perfect merging of the two realities of heaven and earth occurred there. Another way of saying this is that Eden was the place where the natural and the supernatural merged. In our day, we have glimpses of this type of merging as, through the Holy Spirit, we become increasingly aware of the presence of God, His angels, and the reality of His kingdom. Such an atmosphere is often called an *open heaven*. Eden was an open heaven in the fullest possible sense because there was not yet any sin in the garden. Again, it was a place where heaven and earth came together in perfect union in the most beautiful way.

GOD GAVE US HIS NATURE

God, who is perfect love, created us for Himself to love. Love always gives. God first gave of Himself to human beings in that we are made in His image. He bestowed on us His own likeness so that we might enjoy and delight in the uniqueness that is in the person of God alone. Our human design couldn't have been improved upon. It was absolute perfection, as it was modeled after the Creator Himself. As I expressed earlier, everything about us was designed to experience His world of delight, pleasure, and ecstasy, because this world was created for our enjoyment.

It can also be said that we were designed to *host* God, and that interaction with Him is meant to be one of the ways we experience His endless goodness and find our reason for being. Exploring the nature of God is in some ways a discovery of who we are. When the Holy Spirit takes up residence in us, and we are yielded to Him, we naturally mirror the heart and nature of God through our thoughts, attitudes, and actions. The enemy of our souls works hard to tarnish that manifestation of who God is in this world. He does so by trying to persuade us to embrace anxiety, fear, resentment, and regret. Such things lead us down a path that has no answer but repentance. Yielding to God's Word and resisting the devil's plans for us enable us to carry His presence, nature, and assignment into the earth.

> *WE WERE DESIGNED TO HOST GOD, AND THAT INTERACTION WITH HIM IS MEANT TO BE ONE OF THE WAYS WE EXPERIENCE HIS ENDLESS GOODNESS AND FIND OUR REASON FOR BEING.*

GOD GAVE US THE EARTH

In the open heaven called the garden of Eden, God gave Himself in fellowship to Adam and Eve. Interestingly, He also gave the whole earth to this first couple. *"The heaven, even the heavens, are the LORD's; but the earth He has given to the children of men"* (Psalm 115:16 NKJV). With this gift was the responsibility to bring everything outside of the garden into the beauty, wonder, and divine order that was in the garden. The size of Eden was no doubt the exact size Adam and Eve could manage well, as God releases responsibility to *"each according to his own ability"* (Matthew 25:15 NKJV, NASB). They were to extend the borders of the garden until the entire earth was covered with the same beauty, pleasure, and perfect harmony. Taking on such a task of bringing transformation to the globe required them to develop their ability to steward and manage what they had been given charge over. In part, they could do this only by having children who would have children who would have children who would carry the original mandate in their hearts. The goal was to see the entire planet transformed into the wonder of continual ecstasy, pleasure, and delight, all because of human beings' relationship with their Father.

To this day, the earth is humanity's inheritance. The apostle Paul declared this truth when he wrote, *"So then let no one boast in men. For all things belong to you, whether…the world or…things present or things to come; all things belong to you, and you belong to Christ; and Christ belongs to God"* (1 Corinthians 3:21–23 NASB). God's plan to create us in His image and then empower us to co-labor with Him is to bring Him glory. It truly is the most beautiful plan, of which all of creation is in awe.

THE ULTIMATE DREAM: LIVING INSIDE US

It is easy to see how God gave Himself so completely to Adam, and then to Eve, before any act of sin had taken place. But it's even more remarkable to see how He demonstrated His love by giving to them *after* their sin and absolute failure. Following their sin, God continued to give, because He is love. *"For God so loved the world that He gave His only begotten Son, that whoever believes in Him should not perish but have everlasting life*" (John 3:16 NKJV). Love, much like faith, cannot be idle.

It really is amazing to think that sin scarred us so completely that we were disqualified for life as God designed it to be. But the blood of Jesus restored us to the place of delightful sons and daughters of the King so that ongoing fellowship with Father God is possible. Through the blood of Jesus, we are made sinless again. The blood of Jesus enables us to have a perfect connection with the Holy Spirit, God on earth.

Can you imagine it? I can't overemphasize this point: the Creator of the universe put a plan together to spend all eternity living inside those made in His image. To be more specific, He chose to live in the hearts and bodies of those who, through belief in Jesus Christ, have been redeemed from the curse of sin. It is beyond comprehension. God—the almighty One—living in us! We are His eternal dwelling place. We can enjoy a seamless connection with this One who designed us for pleasure and delight, who has chosen to make us His home. His nearness is our joy. As we have seen, the Bible makes it quite clear that fullness of joy is found in the presence of the Lord. (See Psalm 16:11.) And would it not be accurate to say that joy is an expression of someone who has found pleasure and delight?

RESTING UPON

As I began to describe in chapter 3, "Becoming a Resting Place," the Holy Spirit dwells in every believer, but He doesn't always *rest upon* every believer at all times. He rests upon those who are fully yielded to Him, as Jesus was. Giving the Holy Spirit place, giving Him the opportunity to fully express Himself, is what Jesus modeled for us. He taught us how to honor and host this glorious Holy Spirit.

The Holy Spirit lives *in* me for my sake. But He comes *upon* me for the sake of others, to release the Spirit to them. The same Spirit that anoints me for ministry, comforts and directs me for life. When He rests upon me, it is always to bring transformation to my surroundings. Jesus exemplified this truth perfectly. It started at His water baptism, and this aspect of Jesus's story should impact the life of every believer. It is described in this way in John 1:33 (NASB): *"He upon whom you see the Spirit descending and **remaining** upon Him, this is the One who baptizes in the Holy Spirit."* The Holy Spirit came upon Jesus and remained. Although Jesus came to earth with authority, as He was commissioned by the Father, He still needed spiritual power to do all the Father had intended Him to accomplish. His water baptism was the moment when He was clothed with the power of the Holy Spirit. This was both His water baptism and His Spirit baptism. Only after this experience do we see Jesus walking in power for ministry. This may be seen clearly in Luke 3:21–22; 4:1–30. What stands out to me is the emphasis on the Holy Spirit *"remaining"* on Jesus. The implication is that the Spirit of God could have been there one moment and gone the next—in other words, He might not have been a constant or an ever-increasing reality there. But Jesus hosted Him brilliantly, never violating the Spirit of God in any way. He became the perfect resting place for the Holy Spirit.

When I tell this story of Jesus's baptism to groups, I often ask people, "If I had a dove, in the natural, resting upon my shoulder, how would I walk around this room if I wanted it to stay?" "Carefully" is the most frequent answer, and it's accurate. But I'd rather describe it in this way when thinking of my relationship with the Holy Spirit: every step I'd take would be with the dove in mind. Every movement would be to protect and honor what I value most—*Him*.

The lifestyle of Jesus presents us with one continuous story of perfect partnership between a man and the Holy Spirit. Now, lest you think, as some have mistakenly reported, that I don't believe Jesus to be the Son of God, or God in human form, let me affirm this: He is the eternal Son of God! If He is not God, we have no salvation or promise of eternity! But He identified Himself as the Son of Man to illustrate what could be possible for one person who is completely surrendered to the Holy Spirit. The Gospels reveal Jesus to us. But it was the Holy Spirit who enabled the humanity of Jesus to perfectly fulfill the will of the Father on earth.

One of my favorite Bible verses is Acts 10:38 (NASB):

> *You know of Jesus of Nazareth, how God anointed Him with the Holy Spirit and with power, and how He went about doing good and healing all who were oppressed by the devil,* ***for God was with Him.***

When this verse states that "*God was with Him,*" it is not implying that Jesus wasn't God. It is emphasizing the fact that God was with Him in His humanity. This is what made it possible for the Son of Man to do all the Godlike things He did. In fact, at the very beginning of His ministry, Jesus announced that God was with Him:

> *The Spirit of the Lord is upon Me, because He anointed Me to preach the gospel to the poor. He has sent Me to proclaim release to the captives, and recovery of sight to the blind, to set free those who are oppressed, to proclaim the favorable year of the Lord.* (Luke 4:18–19 NASB)

Once more, we see that it was the Holy Spirit upon Jesus that enabled Him to do all that He did. It was because God was with Him that it could be said that He healed "*all who were oppressed by the devil.*" It's not that every person alive was healed or delivered. It was that everyone who came to Him, and everyone the Father directed Him to, received their miracle. No exceptions.

When we read about the three and a half years of Jesus's ministry, we're not always conscious of the fact that we are watching the Holy Spirit at work. But the beautiful thing is that, in those moments, we witness a revelation of the perfect union and manifestation of the Trinity: Father, Son, and Holy Spirit. Through the works and words of Jesus, we see the heart of the Father, manifested through the life, nature, and work of the Holy Spirit.

It is our greatest honor to host this One who longs to reveal and glorify Jesus. And it is Jesus who always points to the Father. Such mystery, beauty, and wonder!

> *THE HOLY SPIRIT LIVES* IN *ME FOR MY SAKE. BUT HE COMES* UPON *ME FOR THE SAKE OF OTHERS.*

MAINTAINING AN ATMOSPHERE FOR HOSTING

We need to maintain an atmosphere in our lives for hosting God's Spirit. As an illustration of this point, remember that Jesus warned of the eternal consequences of blaspheming the Holy Spirit. He said that we could blaspheme Him or the Father, and that could be forgiven, but there's no forgiveness to those who blaspheme the Holy Spirit. (See, for example, Luke 12:10.) This is an incredible mystery to me, and my purpose is not to alarm you but to emphasize that this picture is clear: the Holy Spirit is revered by the Father and the Son and must be revered by us as well. He must not be violated.

The believer's life is lived best by remembering these two approaches to the Holy Spirit, established by the Father: we are not to grieve the Holy Spirit (see Ephesians 4:30), and we are not to quench the Holy Spirit (see 1 Thessalonians 5:19). We grieve Him with wrong behavior, attitudes, thoughts, and plans. This command is focused on our character. We quench Him when we fail to cooperate with Him, stopping the flow of His Word and His power in our lives. This command is focused on the release of power. These are the two legs we stand on: character and power. And one is not more important than the other.

The Holy Spirit is the delicate One, the One with whom we must exert extra caution and care. And yet it is the Holy Spirit who is assigned to live in us. Think of it: broken, despised, sin-filled humanity becomes the dwelling place of the delicate One. (Forgive me; I'm not sure *delicate* is the best word to use, as it could imply weakness, which, of course, is not the case. But hopefully it's close enough to get the picture.) I say this to emphasize the absolutely successful impact of the blood of Jesus applied to a life, which restores that person to the status of humanity in the garden of Eden before sin: being the dwelling place of God. Another important thought in this regard is that we can tell how much God trusts us by recognizing what He has entrusted to us: He has entrusted us with the Holy Spirit Himself. That act, in itself, reveals God's confidence in the power and effectiveness of the blood of Jesus in our lives.

CO-MISSIONED

As we receive God's Spirit (hosting His indwelling) and remain submitted to Him (allowing Him to rest upon us), He will use us to carry out His purposes for the world. We saw earlier that the Scriptures specifically say God was with Jesus as He went about His ministry, doing miraculous works of healing and deliverance. And one of the most fascinating things I have found in my study of the Scriptures is the fact that whenever God revealed to someone that He was with them, it was almost always connected to an impossible assignment for that individual. It's not that God is only with us to help us perform something. That idea doesn't sit well with me, as we know God pursues us for the purpose of relationship. And yet it appears to me that as He walked with Adam in the garden, what Adam would be building and designing could have been at least a part of their conversation.

In the same way, we know that the Holy Spirit is here to comfort, to teach, and to guide us. All of these things are true, and so much more. But again, when God tells a person, "I will be with you," that message is almost always associated with an assignment that person could never complete in the natural. Moses had this experience at the burning bush when God commissioned him:

> *But Moses said to God, "Who am I, that I should go to Pharaoh, and that I should bring the sons of Israel out of Egypt?" And He said,* ***"Certainly I will be with you."*** (Exodus 3:11–12 NASB)

Reading this exchange, it could easily seem as if God had ignored Moses's question, "Who am I?" But I don't think so. To me, it's as if God answered him by saying, "You're the one I want to be with. I am willing to be known as your God." This response was connected to his having been given the responsibility to lead Israel out of Egypt into the "land of promises." Of course, this was an assignment that was impossible from a human standpoint. Moses was to lead slaves into an inheritance more suited for kings (although getting them out of Egypt was much easier than getting Egypt out of them).

Joshua received basically the same assignment that Moses had been given. In fact, God told him, *"No man will be able to stand before you all the days of your life.* ***Just as I have been with Moses, I will be with you****; I will not fail you or forsake you"* (Joshua 1:5 NASB). God commissioned Joshua to take Israel into the promised land, something his predecessor, Moses, was unable to do. And it wasn't about simply walking into an undisturbed land and laying claim to it. No, the land was occupied by people who were bigger, stronger, and greater in number than the Israelites. God Himself said that the enemy's armies were better than Israel's armies. (See Deuteronomy 7:7 NKJV.) That couldn't have been very encouraging to hear from God. But the Lord said He would be with Joshua. That one simple fact outweighed every other strike against the Israelites. God is the X factor.

Later, the Lord spoke similar words to Gideon, assuring him of His presence, and we see that those words were once again tied to an assignment:

> *He* [Gideon] *said to Him, "O Lord, how shall I deliver Israel? Behold, my family is the least in Manasseh, and I am the youngest in my father's house." But the* LORD *said to him, "****Surely I will be with you****, and you shall defeat Midian as one man."* (Judges 6:15–16 NASB)

Gideon was to lead God's people into victory over the surrounding nations that had continually made a mockery of the people of God. They had beaten and plundered the Israelites, driving them into hiding and shame. The people of Israel's sense of self-worth had been shattered. In that context, God called Gideon to be their deliverer, saying He would be with him. So overwhelmed was Gideon over this assignment that he needed confirmation after confirmation that he had heard from God correctly.

In the New Testament, when Jesus appeared to the eleven remaining disciples after His death and resurrection and commissioned them into their reason for being, He told them He would be with them:

> *Go therefore and make disciples of all the nations, baptizing them in the name of the Father and the Son and the Holy Spirit, teaching them to observe all that I commanded you;* ***and lo, I am with you always,*** *even to the end of the age.* (Matthew 28:19–20 NASB)

Those first disciples—and all future disciples—were given an assignment: *"make disciples of all the nations."* This may be the most overwhelming assignment ever given to anyone. All of us as believers inherit this commission. It is ours as much as it was the original Eleven's. But the one thing that makes this assignment doable is the fact that *God is with us*. At this point, it is vital for us to remember that God enables what He commands.

LIVING IN THE POWER OF THE SPIRIT

Hopefully, by now, the point is obvious: when God is revealed to be with someone, it is because He expects something impossible to be done. It's the nature of the gospel. It's the nature of our Father. The gospel invites us to function beyond human ability through the power of the Holy Spirit. And it's the Father who ensures that His requirement of invading the impossible is possible. It's as though, when God is revealed to be with someone, all of heaven lines up to see what we will conquer in His name.

We know that we can do nothing without Jesus. The great tragedy is that we've learned to do nothing *with* Him. But that paradox is changing in this hour, as God is making His "presence assignment" clearly known.

The reality of the Spirit's power moving upon God's people is demonstrated throughout Scripture, in both the Old and New Testament. It was the presence of the Holy Spirit upon Jesus that made the miraculous not only possible but logical. It was to be expected that the impossibilities of life would bow before the Spirit of God that rested on the Son of God. The light of God's power is infinite. Darkness, along with its manifestations of affliction and torment, is finite. Wherever the Holy Spirit demonstrates the absolute majesty of Jesus, victory and liberty are the outcome.

PART TWO:

OUR HELPER

6

THE CROWNING TOUCH

Jesus told His disciples, *"But I tell you the truth, it is to your advantage that I go away; for if I do not go away,* ***the Helper*** *will not come to you; but if I go, I will send Him to you"* (John 16:7 NASB). The Holy Spirit being our Helper is all about enabling us to fulfill our purpose and potential as redeemed members of God's family. The heavenly partnership that is available to us is completely carried out in our relationship with Him. This, then, is the pinnacle of God's creation of us as His co-laborers: God Himself dwelling in us, enabling us to step into the fullness of our purpose in Him. And, as we will see, our relationship with Him has profound implications for our relationships with our family members, other believers, and the people we meet every day.

The list of the Holy Spirit's attributes and roles is endless because we're talking about the nature of the eternal One, the One unlimited in holiness, goodness, beauty, and wonder. The cherished Holy Spirit fills us and assists us in so many ways. In the next few chapters, we will further explore what it means that the Spirit is our Helper, as well as some specific areas in which He assists us: empowering us, interceding on our behalf, speaking truth and wisdom to us, enabling us to hear the Father's voice, inspiring us with unique creativity for the kingdom, and working His fruit and gifts in us so that there is nothing "mundane" about our lives in Christ.

THE HELPER COMPLETES WHAT IS LACKING

Going back to the creation account in Genesis will help us to better understand what God intends when He talks about the Holy Spirit being our Helper. We know that God walked with Adam in the garden in the cool of the evening, and their fellowship was bliss. The world Adam lived in was absolute perfection. And yet it was while Adam was still living in that bliss that the Father said, "*It is not good for the man to be alone; I will make him **a helper** suitable for him*" (Genesis 2:18 NASB). Then God made Eve from one of Adam's ribs to be his wife. (See verses 21–22.) In His wisdom, the Father saw that although everything was perfect and good in Adam's life, it was not yet *complete*, as his potential could not be reached if he remained alone as a human being. Eve was the completion of God's creation.

When God made Eve, it certainly didn't imply He was somehow ineffective or lacking in His ability to fulfill the needs of a relational Adam, or that He Himself wasn't "enough" for Adam. Again, the fellowship between God and Adam was, in itself, perfection. Instead, Adam's capacity, by God's design, was so great that having a relationship with someone in his own likeness would only enhance his walk with God. God would then "hide Himself" within the relationship between husband and wife in such a way that He would be glorified—directly, through His individual relationship with Adam (and Eve), and indirectly, through Adam's treatment of his wife and the value he placed on her.

Jesus stated that at the end of the age, He would say to us, *"As you did it to one of the least of these My brethren, you did it to Me"* (Matthew 25:40 NKJV). In this passage, He emphasizes that He would honor those who had visited others in prison or given even a cup of water in His name to one who was thirsty. (See Matthew 25:31–44.) He taught and modeled such acts of kindness, and He revealed how God essentially hides Himself in the brokenness of humanity, so that every act of compassion we engage in is *like doing it for Jesus Himself.* If God takes personally our dealings with *"the least of these,"* think how much He celebrates it when we properly honor and value the people who are most important in our lives. For Adam, Eve certainly qualified for that status. So then, knowing and honoring Eve was another way for Adam to come to know and honor God. In a very real sense, God hid Himself in Eve for Adam's sake, and He hid Himself in Adam for Eve's sake. Some of our greatest discoveries about God are to be found in the people He places in our lives. And in the ways we learn to receive from other people and serve them in Jesus's name, we learn more about how the Holy Spirit comes alongside us to be our Helper and assist us.

> *GOD ESSENTIALLY HIDES HIMSELF IN THE BROKENNESS OF HUMANITY, SO THAT EVERY ACT OF COMPASSION WE ENGAGE IN IS LIKE DOING IT FOR JESUS HIMSELF.*

THE HELPER EMPOWERS US

When the Father said He was going to give Adam a wife, He described her using the word *"helper."* The expression that has often been used in the church for Eve's role is *helpmate*. Through the years, I've heard many teachings and comments on this word, but while these explanations may have been well-intentioned, they missed the mark miserably.

Historically, the word *helpmate* has been used to describe the "subservient" role of a wife to her husband. Such a poor translation of the word has only added fuel to the ignorance involved in not allowing women to minister.

Eve was not less than Adam, and there wasn't competition between them. Eve was both equal to Adam and complementary to him. Likewise, women are not in a subservient role to men, to be controlled or directed, as though they lacked the spirituality to discern for themselves. Some people approach this idea of "helpmate" as though it were God's punishment to Eve because she ate first from the forbidden fruit. That is nonsense.

Even the concept of *submission*, which has been misinterpreted in our times and applied to women in a similar way, is heaven's plan to give us access to multiplied personal and corporate strength. (See, for example, Ephesians 5:18–21.) A married woman is a helpmate to her husband (not the entire human race of males) in the same way that God is a Helper to His people. In the Old Testament, God is called the "helpmate" of Israel thirteen times. (See, for example, Deuteronomy 33:29; Psalm 33:20.) In being Israel's helpmate, He didn't abdicate the throne to become less than a human. Combining the Hebrew words for *"helper suitable"* (Genesis 2:18 NASB), this beautiful phrase basically means "one enabled to stand face-to-face with another, making up all that may be lacking."[6] We understand this idea as it pertains to our relationship with God. He makes up for what is lacking in us. So true. But it is also true in marital relationships that each spouse helps to make up for what is lacking in the other.

When the Hebrew word rendered as *"helper"* in Genesis 2:18 is used in relation to God in other places in the Old Testament, it normally pertains to His sending military might to assist His people in a crisis. Let's consider this idea the next time we reflect on wives and their role. In a marriage, a wife is a God-assigned "military strategy" to assist the household in victory

6. "Genesis 2:18," NASB Lexicon, Bible Hub, https://biblehub.com/lexicon/genesis/2-18.htm; Jeff A. Benner, "What Is a Help Meet?" Ancient Hebrew Research Center, https://www.ancient-hebrew.org/studies-interpretation/what-is-a-help-meet.htm.

in ways that are often out of reach for the husband. And vice versa: the husband is to assist the wife in eternal conquests, bringing the household into victory. His part is easier to see when we look at Jesus's role with the church, His bride. (See, for example, Ephesians 5:31–32.)

Unity in God between a husband and wife is, in itself, a spiritual military tool for obtaining victory for the glory of God. Perhaps that is why the apostle Peter warned husbands that treating their wives without honor or without an understanding heart would hinder their prayers. (See 1 Peter 3:7.) The way we treat people affects the fruitfulness of our prayer life. Practically speaking, this means we lose our connection of influence with God that bears fruit testifying of our relationship with Him. If the husband would realize that, in his wife, God has raised up someone to make up for what is lacking in him, in a similar way that God Himself makes up for what is lacking in the lives of His people, that one insight would help so many marriages.

The tangible illustration of the relationship between a husband and wife given to us in Scripture is ultimately a picture of the Holy Spirit—the promised One Jesus called "Helper"—and His relationship to God's people. He is the One who stands face-to-face with us, ensuring that we come into the fullness of all that God intended.

In this regard, let us remember that every advancement in life we experience comes with both blessings/rewards and potential dangers. Our relationships with others perfectly illustrate this reality. Having healthy human relationships can be the greatest blessing of our lives, yet handling them incorrectly can bring us much heartache. I want to express what is probably an overly simplistic conclusion that I hope will still serve us well in this context: Our relationship with God is never to take the place of our relationships with other people. Likewise, our relationships with others are never to take the place of our increasingly coming to know God in relationship.

While Jesus teaches that God considers it a service to Him when we serve and honor others in His name, He also warns that we should not love our family members and friends more than we love Him. He says that whoever does this is not worthy of Him. (See Matthew 10:37.) This statement of judgment is for those who put people ahead of their relationship with God. Often, a fear of man is behind that misplaced value. Because Jesus gave such a warning, we know it is possible to love people more than we love God. We also know from what the apostle John taught that if we say we love God but hate our brother, then we are liars. (See 1 John 4:20.) The conclusion is that it is possible to love people more than we love God, but it is impossible to love God without loving people.

Thus, having relationships with both God and other people is essential if we are to fulfill the reason for our existence and be completed by others in profound ways. Living in this way will enable us to fully acknowledge God as our ultimate Helper while allowing other people, including our spouses, to act as essential, complementary supports in our lives. If we could see beyond the obvious, we would recognize that God often reveals Himself to us through other people. We need to be alert to how the Holy Spirit is working in this way. Again, the beauty of this mystery is that God will often hide Himself in our simple interactions with family members, friends, and even strangers. Staying in awe of Him helps us to benefit from these people-encounters in ways that sometimes equal the significant moments we have with God in worship and prayer.

We have seen that, as our Helper, God fights on behalf of His people. The Holy Spirit uses all the tools in His arsenal to draw us to the Father and conform us to the image of His Son, Jesus Christ. And one of the specific ways in which the Spirit does this is through interceding for us and guiding us in our own prayers.

KINGDOM PRAYING

I'm sure that if Jesus were sitting right in front of you, you—like me—would want Him to teach you many things, because this world has never seen a teacher like Him. His perception of the Father and His heart impact me deeply. I would want to know more about those aspects. I'd love to know what He was thinking right before He walked on the water during a fierce storm (see, for example, Matthew 14:22–33) or how He knew the young girl who had died would live again when He took her by the hand and told her to stand up (see Mark 5:21–24; 35–43). It would be amazing to hear Him talk about heaven itself. That fascinates me no end. And how did the voice of God manifest to Him? Most of us could probably write a book of questions we'd like to have answered and knowledge we'd love to learn from the greatest Teacher who ever lived. And yet those who were always with Him, who were the most acquainted with His life and ministry, only asked to be taught one thing: how to pray. Understanding what Jesus taught about prayer will help us to align our prayers with God's will and the leading of the Holy Spirit.

> *Now it came to pass, as He was praying in a certain place, when He ceased, that one of His disciples said to Him, "Lord, teach us to pray, as John also taught his disciples." So He said to them, "When you pray, say: 'Our Father in heaven, hallowed be Your name. Your kingdom come. Your will be done on earth as it is in heaven. Give us day by day our daily bread. And forgive us our sins, for we also forgive everyone who is indebted to us. And do not lead us into temptation, but deliver us from the evil one.'"* (Luke 11:1–4 NKJV)

Jesus's response to this request was to teach His followers "the Disciples' Prayer" (this seems a more appropriate title to me than "the Lord's Prayer" since it is a model for us). I don't think Jesus said this prayer over and over again when He prayed all night on the mountain. (See, for example, Luke 6:12–16.) Neither do I think He was giving His disciples a prayer that would limit their hearts' expression to the Father, thus creating a religious routine. I actually love praying this prayer in Matthew's version. (See Matthew 6:9–13.) But in my way of thinking, this model prayer was given to us to highlight appropriate priorities we need to keep in mind whenever we approach the Father. More specifically, we see the following priorities in the prayer Jesus taught: worshipping the Father, praying for heaven's reality to invade earth now, acknowledging the need for provision, embracing a commitment to live a lifestyle of forgiveness, and realizing we are in a spiritual battle and thus asking for protection.

These are highlights of intentional prayer. They represent the basic needs of every believer. We are to use them as a guide as we allow the Holy Spirit to lead us in our prayers. But while following this focus in our prayers is important and effective, there is so much more that we need to know and do, and this again is where our Helper makes up for what we lack.

In John 14–16, Jesus unveils the ultimate feature of our design in God's image in that, with the Holy Spirit living in us, we are positioned to *ask for anything, and it will be done*. (See John 15:7.) We can pray for all aspects of God's heavenly kingdom to come to earth and see them fulfilled through the power of His Spirit. What I find interesting is that, in those three chapters, where Jesus promises His disciples four times that their desires will be fulfilled (see John 14:13–14; 15:7, 16; 16:23–24), He also states that the Holy Spirit is called the Helper and would be given to them by the Father (see John 14:16, 26; 15:26; 16:7). This title for the Spirit is mentioned four times in these three chapters. I don't think this is a coincidence. Four times, the disciples are invited to ask for anything, and it would be done. And four times, the Holy Spirit is described as the Helper.

Dreaming big is supposed to be a result of our yielded relationship with the Holy Spirit and His influence on our future. Jesus is the One who said, "Abide in Me, and let My words abide in you, and anything you ask for will be done for you." (See John 15:7.) Is it humility for us to pray, "Not my will, but Yours" (see Luke 22:42) in this situation? Is it humility to say, "God, I want nothing but You. I only want Your will to be done"? Before you answer, consider again that four times in three chapters, Jesus tells His disciples that anything they desire will be done for them. In John 16:24 (NKJV), He says, *"Ask, and you will receive, that your joy may be full."* Receiving answers to our prayers and desires is the key to fullness of joy. The pathway to such significance in prayer is learning to pray the will of God. We become shaped in that process—so much so that He wants to hear our will! It's a scary invitation, for sure. And yet it is part of the mystery and paradox of the gospel life, where we die to live (see, for example, John 12:24–25), and we go low to rise high (see, for example, Luke 14:11).

These verses about receiving what we ask for all look good to us on paper, as we instinctively know we must live in humility to represent Jesus well. But if He commands me to bring my desires to Him, and I don't do it because I think it seems selfish, can that be called obedience? Can disobedience ever be considered humility? Jesus's invitation to ask for what we desire gives us a chance to prove that His felt presence in our lives, with the corresponding value we place on His Word, is to produce desires in us that move Him. To fall short in His invitation to ask Him to fulfill our desires and see things be done for His glory is to embrace false humility as a virtue.

Most of us become nauseated over the false expression of the gospel that is exhibited when people construct ministries that are really personal empires, built around selfish pleasure, and call it God's will. I understand such a reaction to this error. Yet if our responses to error are not guided by the Holy Spirit, they often create other errors. In our attempts to be humble, we can fail to become the people God designed us to be. This is not humility because it avoids the most challenging kind of obedience: the kind that can be misunderstood by our critics. A fear of man inspires many people to embrace an anemic gospel in the name of humility and never become what God intended. Thus, the fear of man can masquerade as both wisdom and humility.

There have been times, too many for me to count, when my will was not God's will at all. Although He invites me to pray my will, He reserves the right to say no to any prayer that would undermine my design and purpose in Him. He is too good a Father to ignore His perfect plan and instead yield to our uninformed, misguided, or self-serving ones.

Jesus practiced this challenging kind of obedience to God when, at the age of twelve, He stayed behind in Jerusalem after a family pilgrimage there. When Joseph and Mary noticed He was missing from their group and finally found Him at the temple, discussing the Scriptures with the teachers of the law, He told them, *"Did you not know that I must be about my Father's business?"* (Luke 2:49 NKJV). Or what about the time Jesus left a crowd of spiritually hungry people after ministering to them and feeding them a meal, in order to go up on a mountain to pray? (See, for example, Mark 6:33–46.) We've done a good job of sanitizing this story, but if you were in that crowd of desperate people who were *"like sheep without a shepherd"* (verse 34 NASB), and if you had additional needs you wanted Jesus to address, how would you have felt when He sent you and everyone else away? Or what about the fact that Jesus announced to His disciples that He was going to leave them to return to the Father? It seems rather obvious that the disciples didn't see this news the way Jesus did—as something beneficial—at least initially. So, wasn't it rather self-serving of Jesus to disappear on His parents during a trip, send needy crowds away, and leave His disciples in order to return to heaven? Of course, we know it wasn't self-serving because He was obeying the leading of the Holy Spirit in fulfillment of God's purposes, but that perspective is easier on this side of the equation. Although we don't understand all of God's ways when we're in the middle of a difficult or perplexing situation, we are asked to fully trust Him and still request what we desire.

We know that Jesus didn't promote a self-centered gospel where we use a magic wand to make all our wishes come to pass. That would be the opposite of all He taught and illustrated. And yet by telling His disciples to ask for what they wanted, He drew them into something that was far outside their understanding or experience—something beyond even the point of reference of much of Israel's history. Although God would carry out His purposes in His timing and wisdom, He was still interested in their desires! And this is the essential point we so often miss in our relationship with God.

As I wrote earlier, we know we can do nothing without Him, but our problem is that we've learned to do nothing *with* Him for fear of getting it wrong. It is time for the Father to be revealed through a group of yielded believers whose dreams take them into the impossible for the glory of God.

> *DREAMING BIG IS SUPPOSED TO BE A RESULT OF OUR YIELDED RELATIONSHIP WITH THE HOLY SPIRIT AND HIS INFLUENCE ON OUR FUTURE.*

THE HELPER INTERCEDES FOR US

The apostle Paul addresses the issue of effective prayer in Romans 8, which, to me, is one of the most fulfilling and inviting chapters in the whole Bible. There is so much to glean from this chapter, especially as it pertains to the person of the Holy Spirit. But here's the passage I want us to look at:

> *Likewise the Spirit also helps in our weaknesses. For we do not know what we should pray for as we ought, but* ***the Spirit Himself makes intercession for us*** *with groanings which cannot be uttered. Now He who searches the hearts knows what the mind of the Spirit is, because He makes intercession for the saints according to the will of God....* ***Christ*** *who died, and furthermore is also risen,...is even at the right hand of God,* ***who also makes intercession for us.***
>
> (Romans 8:26–27, 34 NKJV)

This is a remarkable passage. Paul acknowledges that we don't know what we're doing when we pray. Knowing our priorities in prayer isn't enough. It is almost as if Jesus, in wanting to fully answer the one request of His own disciples, gave the Holy Spirit to believers as the Teacher of prayer and worship. We know that one of the main influences of the Spirit of God is that of a teacher. And when we speak in tongues—in an unknown language enabled by the Holy Spirit—the tongues can be either prayer or worship. We see this combination reflected in Romans 8. While I don't necessarily believe that the *"groanings"* of the Spirit that Paul speaks about in this passage are the same as praying in tongues, I do think they are a description of the Holy Spirit praying through a surrendered believer. In Galatians, Paul makes an extreme statement that I believe refers to intercessory prayer: *"My children, with whom I am again* ***in labor*** *until Christ is formed in you"* (Galatians 4:19 NASB). The *"labor"* spoken of in this verse is a picture of deep prayer. It involves groanings—beyond words.

I can't pretend to understand all of this, but I can delight in it. Consider how remarkable it is that both the Holy Spirit and Jesus pray. And They pray for us!

Now look at the verse that is sandwiched in between the ones describing the two great Intercessors, Jesus and the Holy Spirit: *"And we know that all things work together for good to those who love God, to those who are the called according to His purpose"* (Romans 8:28 NKJV). No wonder *"all things work together for good."* Our legal Advocate and our Redeemer both appear before the Father, pleading our case!

WHY DO WE NEED TO PRAY?

One might ask, if the Holy Spirit and Jesus already know the will of God, then why do They need to pray? Or further yet, why do *we* need to pray? God has all power. He is sovereign and requires no one to complete Him. His will is supreme, and He can make anything happen that He wants to happen. But will He? If God can make anything happen that He wants to happen, are the prayers of both the Holy Spirit and Jesus a formality? Are they made merely to provide us with an example to follow? Are they actually necessary?

I don't have answers to these questions that I feel fully satisfied to give, except to say that if the Holy Spirit and Jesus need to pray to see the Father's will done on earth, how much more do we need to pray to see it done?

God could remove all evil from the earth, but He would have to destroy every sinner in the process. He could make it so that all human beings serve Him, but to do so, He'd have to remove our free will and/or make every other option in life so immediately painful that we would choose Him. But such a robotic state in humans would be a dishonor to Him. He made us all in His image, with the ability to choose for ourselves.

Our prayers are not only one of the ultimate expressions of our co-laboring with God, but they are also manifestations of our free will, in which we choose to align with God's will. Many of the things God desires will never be done without the prayers of His people. Thus, it's spiritual irresponsibility to know the will of God and assume it will happen simply because God wants it to. He desires all people to come to repentance (see 1 Timothy 2:3–4), but they don't all come to this place. People after His own heart must pray for His desires. (See, for example, Acts 13:22.) This opportunity is the ultimate gift of God: to have access to His throne room in Jesus's name, to influence what happens on earth. It's an invitation given to us all. My deep desire is that we will respond to the divine cry, go through the open door—Christ Jesus—and pray through the Holy Spirit. Let us pray that the heart of God will be more fully manifest on the earth. Let us listen and pray, look and pray.

We read in James 5:16 (NASB), *"Therefore, confess your sins to one another, and pray for one another so that you may be healed. The effective prayer of a righteous man can accomplish much."* This verse is followed by a reference to Elijah's earnest prayers for rain. (See verses 17–18.) The point is, token prayers get token answers. Convenient prayers get convenient answers. But intercession is a call to pray as though lives depend on it. Because they do. Effective prayers can accomplish much.

So, why pray? Because Jesus prays, and we are His followers. He is our Master, our Leader. Can we claim to follow Him and not pray? (See, for example, Matthew 10:24.)

So, why pray? Because the Holy Spirit prays. He leads us and empowers us. For what? To represent Jesus well on earth, demonstrating His character, His power, and His redemptive purposes. The Holy Spirit is exactly like Jesus. And He always prays the perfect will of God. He is the One who searches the mind of God, getting all the information needed to lead us well. Plus, He is the One who, through the inspired Word, commanded us to *"pray without ceasing"* (1 Thessalonians 5:17 NKJV, NASB). This is what it is like to be led by the Spirit and to have a lifestyle of prayer. One of the reasons praying in tongues is so wonderful is that when we do so, we are always praying the perfect will of God because the One who searches the mind of God is praying through us.

You would think that if God were ever to have independently enforced His will to make sure something happened, it would have been at the birth of His Son. And yet we see that before Jesus was born, Anna and Simeon prayed for God to send the Messiah. (See Luke 2:25–38.) Even the return of Christ is being preceded by prayer, and the Bible says, *"The Spirit and the bride say, 'Come!'"* (Revelation 22:17, various translations). The most important moments in history were preceded by prayer because, by God's design, prayer is absolutely necessary to the fulfillment of His will.

Let me illustrate this point in this way: If I am the owner of a home, and you are renting that home from me, I cannot enter it at will. Even though it is legally mine, I must have your permission to go in. Similarly, the world is the Lord's. It's all His. (See, for example, Psalm 24:1.) But He put human beings in charge of the earth, and He will not violate His choice or His delegated authority by entering into it unasked. He enters at our invitation. It's called prayer. It is how we partner with God to see His redemptive purpose revealed to this world. Just like Jesus and the Holy Spirit, we must pray.

Thus, the Holy Spirit is the key to our fulfilling God's design for us to obtain answers to prayer. His praying through us is sure to obtain the breakthroughs we were born for, as there are aspects of the Father's nature that will not be revealed in the earth apart from the fulfilled desires of His people. It is this design that reveals Him as the heavenly Father—our Father. The very fact that it is the *Holy* Spirit who directs this process assures, through His influence, that these are sanctified desires, born out of a sanctified people. This combination is what our planet of orphans—those who have not yet come to know their heavenly Father—is longing to see, although most do not yet realize it.

John Wesley once said, "God does nothing but in answer to prayer."[7] Prayer is how we display our responsibility to oversee a planet that God has put us in charge of. It is through prayer guided and empowered by the Holy Spirit that we demonstrate our connection to a perfect Father who longs to bring about His purposes in a broken world.

7. Charles Wesley, *A Plain Account of Christian Perfection* (New Kensington, PA: Whitaker House, 2015), 127.

7

THE BEAUTY OF HIS VOICE

Jesus is the Word of God made flesh. (See John 1:14.) His very being carries His message, and He has much to say. Sometimes He speaks through His voice—whether it is expressed in a still, small way (see 1 Kings 19:12) that we internally discern; through what may seem like unusual coincidences; in riddles or parables; audibly; or in other ways. Sometimes He speaks through His manifest presence. As the Word of God, there is no limit to the ways in which He can speak to us. We have to adjust to Him and learn when and how He is speaking. I suspect we will be doing this throughout eternity!

Remember that when Jesus was on earth, His every action and word was at the Father's direction and was empowered by the Holy Spirit. Theirs was a divine symphony, each playing His own part, each bringing honor and delight to the other. It was perfect unity, purpose, and delight.

Jesus accurately illustrated the Father through His surrender to Him, His radical obedience to Him, and His boldness to fulfill God's will—even to His death on the cross. As I described earlier, He did all of this by living dependently upon the Holy Spirit; everything Jesus did revealed the heart of the Father through the working of the Spirit. Jesus stated, *"He who has seen Me has seen the Father"* (John 14:9 NKJV, NASB). Seeing one person of the Trinity is truly seeing all three. Recognizing this reality helps us to glean a better understanding of the Holy Spirit. He may be seen everywhere Jesus is seen.

GOD'S UNMEASURABLE THOUGHTS TOWARD US

The Holy Spirit comes to us from eternity with unlimited imagination, dreams, and plans. These aspects are beyond all human intelligence and brilliance, are motivated by a heart of love for us, and are measured by God's compassion and affection. Quite frankly, His thoughts and plans are beyond our capacity to fully experience, let alone comprehend. Again, to explore this vast universe called the mind of God will take all of eternity.

Such wonders are best explored through the heart. A surrendered heart easily receives and is never able to take the glory for itself. True worship is a place of deep surrender, a response to a God who is always good toward us. As a worshipper, King David experienced this deep spiritual well, setting a new "high-water mark" for human understanding of the heart of God. It only seems right that the man known for having a "heart after God" (see 1 Samuel 13:14) would be the one to clearly see God's heart for us, strikingly described in Psalm 139.

David discovered something about the reality of God's thoughts toward us that is impossible to fully grasp. But that is part of its beauty. It's the value of mystery, the unlimited expression that comes from a perfectly loving Father. We often stare up at the sky, looking at the stars, the

Milky Way, the moon, meteors—all of it beheld in wonder, yet none of it completely comprehended. If I could fully understand any part of God's nature and purpose, He really wouldn't be all that noteworthy. I would end up with a god who was about my size. Very unimpressive. On the other hand, through the Holy Spirit, we are invited to explore the inexhaustible resources of our Creator's love, ideas, and promises. David spoke of God's vast landscape of thoughts when he said:

> *For You formed my inward parts; You wove me in my mother's womb. I will give thanks to You, for I am fearfully and wonderfully made; wonderful are Your works, and* ***my soul knows it very well****. My frame was not hidden from You, when I was made in secret, and skillfully wrought in the depths of the earth; Your eyes have seen my unformed substance; and in Your book were all written the days that were ordained for me, when as yet there was not one of them.* ***How precious also are Your thoughts*** *to me, O God! How vast is the sum of them! If I should count them,* ***they would outnumber the sand****. When I awake, I am still with You.* (Psalm 139:13–18 NASB)

God's thoughts are beyond grand, and their significance cannot be measured. Interestingly, our inner man is more conscious of God's thoughts and ways than we often realize. Accordingly, the psalmist confesses, "*My soul knows it very well.*" God's thoughts about us outnumber the grains of sand on all the seashores of the earth. And considering that there are about sixty thousand miles of sandy beaches on the planet, we're dealing with another incomprehensible concept. Let me illustrate the magnitude of this statement.

If we were to measure one cubic inch of sandy beach based on an average-sized grain of sand, we would find a little over three hundred thousand grains. That adds up to four billion grains of sand in a cubic foot.[8] Multiply

8. "Coast," Britannica, updated July 13, 2024, https://www.britannica.com/science/coast#ref115982; "Taking Stock of the World's Sandy Beaches," Earth Observatory, NASA, https://earthobservatory.nasa.gov/images/92507/taking-stock-of-the-worlds-sandy-beaches; "How Many Grains of Sand Are in One Square Inch?" Answers, August 17, 2023, https://math.answers.com/other-math/How_many_grains_of_sand_are_in_one_square_inch; "How Many Sand Grains Is in a Cubit Foot?" Answers, April 28, 2022, https://math.answers.com/other-math/How_many_sand_grains_is_in_a_cubic_ft.

that by the miles of shoreline for one beach, with depths ranging from a few inches to over a hundred feet. And then consider that there are about sixty thousand miles of sandy shorelines on the earth. That's a lot of sand, representing the magnitude of thoughts, ideas, and dreams that God has for us. Certainly, we can see from this illustration that it will take all of eternity to explore and fulfill such dreams. According to Jeremiah, God's thoughts toward us are for our well-being, not our adversity: *"For I know the thoughts that I think toward you, says the Lord, thoughts of peace and not of evil, to give you a future and a hope"* (Jeremiah 29:11 NKJV). It is safe to say that we have been on God's mind for a long time. Each person who is born again can anticipate the adventure of a lifetime, exploring the depths of God's mind for us for all eternity.

To be born again is to be born of the Holy Spirit. (See John 3:5–6, 8.) Even our conversion is a display of His wonder-working power, as it is the actual power of Jesus's resurrection that makes us a new creation. Directing our thoughts to be consistent with what Jesus has done in us is one of the most important aspects of our Christian life, especially because our thinking is the area of our lives that we most often ignore or abuse. Paul exhorted us to this end in Romans 6:11 (NASB): *"Even so consider yourselves to be dead to sin, but alive to God in Christ Jesus."* In other words, because of the death and resurrection of Christ, and because of what the Holy Spirit has done for all of us who believe, think of yourself in this way: "I am dead to sin and alive to God in Christ Jesus." Dead people do no wrong. Our thinking is to be shaped, formed, and instructed by what the Holy Spirit has done for us—and this renewed thinking will influence our actions.

HEAVENLY SEARCH ENGINE

The greatest "search engine" in the universe is the Holy Spirit. And the greatest reservoir of information and insight is the mind of God, which is, in itself, eternal and unlimited in scope and ever-expanding. The Holy Spirit searches the Father's mind, looking for specific thoughts that will conform us more closely to the likeness of Jesus, with greater strength and faith. Merely increasing our self-confidence is never the goal, as the "self" provides very limited progress, if any. But when we receive the revelation of God's mind for us, we find out who we are and who He has made us to be. Just learning His thoughts about us is liberating. We discover our true selves, as we are in Christ, in the revelation of who God is. And that is our strength.

The apostle Paul addresses this theme in a letter to the church of Corinth:

> *But as it is written: "Eye has not seen, nor ear heard, nor have entered into the heart of man the things which God has prepared for those who love Him." But God has revealed them to us through His Spirit. For the Spirit searches all things, yes, the deep things of God. For what man knows the things of a man except the spirit of the man which is in him? Even so no one knows the things of God except the Spirit of God. Now we have received, not the spirit of the world, but the Spirit who is from God, that we might know the things that have been freely given to us by God.* (1 Corinthians 2:9–12 NKJV)

The first thing to take note of in this passage is the statement in verse 9 that what God has prepared for us has never even entered our minds. Not even in our wildest and most extreme dreams have we ever approached the wonder and beauty of what God has created for us. Paul then says that God has revealed these things *through His Spirit*. What has always been beyond the reach of human intellect and imagination is now within reach of anyone who learns to hear the voice of the Holy Spirit. You've heard the phrase "It's too good to be true." In our case, "It's so good, it must be true."

The Holy Spirit is the agent of mystery, introducing us to our eternal purpose of discovering the things of God that have already been given to us by inheritance. The Spirit is constantly trying to help us to receive and utilize our inheritance, which becomes manifest in greater measure every time He speaks. He always works in us for the glory of God.

> ***WHEN WE RECEIVE THE REVELATION OF GOD'S MIND FOR US, WE FIND OUT WHO WE ARE AND WHO HE HAS MADE US TO BE.***

IN WHAT WAYS DOES GOD SPEAK?

I think each of us wishes we heard from God better than we do. Several times, I've noticed that when someone says they want to hear God's voice better, another person will respond, "Stop looking up. Just look down at your Bible. He spoke through Scripture." And while I think this is a cute response, as the Scriptures are the basis for our hearing from God, it does little to answer the cry of the heart for a relationship of interaction with a Father who loves us dearly. It is in our DNA to long to hear His voice in a personal way. Our life in Christ started because He individually called us to Himself, and we responded to that call.

We live because God speaks. Life on earth began with His voice. He who spoke the world into being has called us to Himself and given us eternal life. If God had not called us to Himself, we could not know Him. Thankfully, He speaks to us all very generously, saying, "Whosoever will may come." (See Revelation 22:17.) But having the faith to respond to His dealings with the outcome of absolute surrender to Christ starts with an internal struggle to leave sin and follow the Son of God. The faith to believe Him for our salvation came the moment we responded to His call, His voice. He first loved us; then we loved Him. He first spoke to us; then we responded to Him. He initiates; we either receive or reject.

God speaks to us in various ways, among them subtle ideas to our minds and either loud or soft communications. Let's look at these means and then explore how we can best prepare ourselves to hear Him.

SUBTLY, IN OUR THOUGHTS AND IMPRESSIONS

The voice of the Lord is often an internal, familiar voice that introduces a thought or insight we had not previously considered. What comes to us is usually not something we would have thought of on our own. We used to half-jokingly say, "You know when God has spoken to you because you have a thought that is better than one you could think up yourself." Yet people often take credit for the thoughts they receive in such moments, believing they just accidentally stumbled on an idea. I don't think this mistake comes from arrogance as much as from ignorance. They just don't understand how subtle God's voice can be. He speaks to our inner man, interweaving His mind into our experiences, surroundings, and feelings in a most mysterious way.

Often, someone will say, "I can't hear God's voice, but I do feel His peace." They rarely seem to realize that the peace they feel *is* His voice. Since He is the Word of God, His presence is a manifestation of His voice. That concept just hasn't reached our minds yet. My personal conviction is that He often deposits insights into our spirit-man that are to be brought out in the coming hours or days. We must learn to always stay tender to God—not just when there's a crisis or an urgent need.

DURING WORSHIP

The key here is to affectionately draw near to God in worship, knowing that during our worship, He is depositing the specifics of His Word deeply into our hearts. He will then bring these truths to the surface at the moment they are most needed. The Holy Spirit is the great worship leader in heaven, as all worship is in spirit. (See John 4:24.) Worship is a Holy Spirit activity. As such, it is one of the most practical ways to learn to recognize His presence and, in doing so, learn His heart and mind. The affectionate expression of worship is a way of demonstrating our surrender to God while encountering Him.

The bliss, the perfect pleasure and union, between worshippers and God might best be represented by the meaning of one of the Greek words for *worship* used in the New Testament: "to kiss towards."[9] It implies an affectionate response to God. We have the distinct privilege of ministering to God directly. A priest, the position to which all New Testament believers are called (see, for example, Revelation 1:5–6), is one who ministers directly to the Lord. I believe that, for this reason, many songs have been written in the last thirty years or so that speak directly *to* God, not just *about* Him, or even about important concepts in theology, although both of those aspects are important as well. Ministering to God implies a one-on-one relationship, even when we are in a crowd.

---

9. *Strong's*, G4352, Blue Letter Bible Lexicon, https://www.blueletterbible.org/lexicon/g4352/kjv/tr/0-1/.

Thus, sometimes we hear the voice of the Lord through inspired thoughts, ideas, or impressions, whether during the course of our everyday lives or in our times of prayer or worship. This may not be as direct a means of communication as we might wish for. Yet God has access to everything in our present, past, and future, and He will use all of it to bring about His purposes in us.

When people realize that what they thought was their idea actually came from God, it strengthens their faith immensely. Knowing you hear from God is more encouraging and rewarding than thinking everything comes to you because you are a genius with creative ideas. Even where true natural genius is involved, so is God. It's much more gratifying to see how we fit into the bigger picture of co-laboring with God than it is to fulfill the demands of our ego. Knowing we've heard the voice of God is both humbling and exalting at the same time. It's another one of those apparent contradictions, or paradoxes, that exist only in the kingdom of God.

AUDIBLY

God may also sometimes speak to us audibly. This form of communication is much less common, but it does occur. I've heard the audible voice of God twice. It is unmistakable and impossible to miss, although we may need to discern what we are hearing. A biblical example of this is when God spoke to the prophet Samuel when he was just a boy:

> *Now the boy Samuel was ministering to the LORD before Eli. And word from the LORD was rare in those days, visions were infrequent. It happened at that time as Eli was lying down in his place (now his eyesight had begun to grow dim and he could not see well), and the lamp of God had not yet gone out, and Samuel was lying down in the temple of the LORD where the ark of God was, that the LORD called Samuel; and he said, "Here I am." Then he ran to Eli and said, "Here I am, for you called me." But he said, "I did not call, lie down again." So he went and lay down. The LORD called yet again, "Samuel!" So Samuel arose and went to Eli and said, "Here I am, for you called me." But he*

> *answered, "I did not call, my son, lie down again." Now Samuel did not yet know the* Lord*, nor had the word of the* Lord *yet been revealed to him. So the* Lord *called Samuel again for the third time. And he arose and went to Eli and said, "Here I am, for you called me." Then Eli discerned that the* Lord *was calling the boy. And Eli said to Samuel, "Go lie down, and it shall be if He calls you, that you shall say, 'Speak,* Lord*, for Your servant is listening.'"* (1 Samuel 3:1–9 NASB)

God speaks in countless other ways. But these three—hearing from God subtly in our thoughts, receiving from Him through worship, and hearing from Him audibly—are enough for now as we continue on our relational journey with the Holy Spirit.

PREPARING OUR HEARTS TO HEAR GOD

How do we prepare our hearts to hear what God is saying to us through the Holy Spirit? We can do this in the following ways: by actively seeking what He desires to share with us; anticipating His voice; reflecting on what He has already revealed to us; living in His rest rather than allowing sin, anxiety, or distractions to block His voice; and receiving His words even when they are perplexing to us and we don't fully understand their meaning.

SEEK WHAT GOD HAS HIDDEN FOR US

"It is the glory of God to conceal a matter, but the glory of kings is to search out a matter." Solomon made this declaration in Proverbs 25:2 (NKJV, NASB). The beautiful part of this reality is discovering that God hides things *for* us, not *from* us. They are there to be searched for. The second part of the verse says that it's the glory of kings *"to search out a matter."* In other words, our royalty in Christ is never more clearly pronounced than when we live with the realization that the mysteries of God's kingdom are there for our discovery. Perhaps we could state it in this way: the muscle of royalty is developed through its use in pursuing the mysteries of God. These mysteries are the things that He has set aside for our discovery. It's the adventurous heart of a child that best represents the kingly in God's

kingdom. Children are always in pursuit of more. *"Do not fear, little flock, for it is your Father's good pleasure to give you the kingdom"* (Luke 12:32 NKJV).

> ***OUR ROYALTY IN CHRIST IS NEVER MORE CLEARLY PRONOUNCED THAN WHEN WE LIVE WITH THE REALIZATION THAT THE MYSTERIES OF GOD'S KINGDOM ARE THERE FOR OUR DISCOVERY.***

ANTICIPATE HIS VOICE

A number of years ago, my grandson Judah—who was only five years old at the time—went to his mother, my daughter Leah, and said, "You will have a baby girl, and you will call her Bella." What Leah and her husband, Gabe, had not told him was that, although they already had two wonderful sons, they wanted to have another child; they were hoping for a girl, and the name they had picked for her was Isabella. Leah soon discovered she was pregnant. She and Gabe took Judah with them when they went to get a sonogram. While she was performing the sonogram, the nurse asked if they wanted to know the sex of the baby. They said yes! She told them it definitely was a girl. Both Gabe and Leah excitedly rejoiced, while Judah showed no emotion. They said, "Judah, did you hear? It is a girl." To which he responded, almost with disgust, "Mom, I told you it was a girl."

Later, Gabe sat down with Judah and asked him how he had known this. His response was that God had told him. Gabe said, "I know that. But how did He speak to you?" His answer was brilliant and so true: "Sometimes God speaks very loudly. And sometimes He speaks very softly. This time, it was very soft." This insight came from a five-year-old who was open to hear God's voice.

I've heard the still, small voice of God countless times. And I am certain I have missed it many times—sometimes out of my resolve to do my own will, and sometimes because of anxiety or fear that dominated the moment. Often, God's still, small voice has to be anticipated in order to be heard. It's so easy to miss it or talk yourself out of the impression you have just received from God. Since words become presence, recognizing a word from God will assist you in discerning when He is at work. Jesus said it this way: "My words to you are Spirit, and they are life." (See John 6:63.) Words from the Spirit manifest God's presence, and His presence gives life. That is the economy of God's heart and mind. It is manifest more often than we think. Learning to "lean in," or pay close attention, helps.

Let me give you a simple illustration. Let's say I'm going to the store to buy groceries. Before I leave, I notice some cash I have left on the countertop. I then have the thought that I should bring the cash with me. But I think it through and realize that would be unnecessary because I always pay for the groceries with my credit card, which I pay off at the end of the month. However, when I get to the store, I have a strong impression that I should help an apparently homeless man who is in front of the store. I have no cash with me, but there is an ATM nearby, so I obtain the cash I need. But in that moment, I realize that God had earlier given me a subtle prompting that I should have paid more attention to. This illustration does not describe a serious or life-or-death situation. But most of life is like that: Simple. Practical. And always fulfilling if we are following God's guidance through the Holy Spirit.

I am so thankful that God is the God of second chances. Most of us are alive because of them. His second chances are a wonderful manifestation of His grace. But it is foolish to think that God will automatically repeat Himself if we miss what He said the first time. This assumption has led many people to unintentionally "tempt God" by assuming He'll work in a certain way when He actually owes us nothing. This is a sober reality to contemplate, especially as we mature. Both the blessings of hearing and the cost of not hearing increase. These costs are not punishment—they are the proper way for us to be trained as stewards of all things concerning the kingdom. We are being trained for ruling and reigning with God for all eternity. Everything in His kingdom increases through proper stewardship.

REMEMBER WHAT GOD HAS ALREADY SPOKEN

One of the ways people often punish someone else is by refusing to speak to or acknowledge the other person. We call this behavior "giving the silent treatment." God is often silent toward us in the sense that He does not use obvious, overt ways of speaking and communicating, but that does not mean He is giving us the silent treatment as a punishment. His silence takes some getting used to, especially when our level of hunger for Him has increased dramatically. God is often silent because He has already spoken to us (perhaps in the subtle way described above), and it's up to us to remember/recall/discover what He has said in a previous season of our lives. Often, we face challenges that He has prepared us for, but we don't feel ready because we haven't held on with faith to the things He has previously spoken.

Mary the mother of Jesus is my favorite example of someone who exercised the discipline of both hearing and remembering:

When Mary was greeted by the angel and received the news that she was favored by God (thereafter hearing that she would be the mother of the Messiah), *"she was very perplexed at this statement, and kept pondering what kind of salutation this was"* (Luke 1:29 NASB).

At Jesus's birth, after hearing the shepherds describe how the angels appeared to them and what they said about Jesus, *"Mary treasured all these things, pondering them in her heart"* (Luke 2:19 NASB).

After Mary and Joseph searched for Jesus for three days and found Him in the temple, talking with the religious leaders, "[Jesus] *went down with them* [Mary and Joseph] *and came to Nazareth, and He continued in subjection to them; and His mother treasured all these things in her heart"* (Luke 2:51 NASB).

A number of years ago, my wife and I were given some very expensive glassware. I keep it in a cabinet, out of reach for daily use. It is for special occasions only. It's certainly not what I would give to my grandchildren when they want a drink of water. It's not that I don't value these younger family members. It's that I don't want the glasses to break because I have put them in the hands of someone unprepared to care for them properly. I don't want to give my grandchildren a responsibility that they have no ability to steward well. It would be unfair to them.

The cabinet where these glasses are stored has glass doors, which makes it possible for us to look at them anytime. On top of that, there are lights built into the cabinet to draw attention to the beauty of the glassware. I have shown the glasses to friends who come to visit my home, and I use them if the occasion seems appropriate. The point is, they are treasured and used only for special events.

Mary treasured God's words to her, including those spoken to her by Jesus. She "pondered them in her heart," which implies she mulled over them in her heart and mind, day after day. As the mystery of the life of Jesus unfolded, Mary no doubt recognized that it was the Lord who had prepared her for the events Jesus was about to experience through the word of the Lord. It implies that she highly valued the words she had been given and did not consider them a random addition to her life; in fact, they gave her a central focus for why she was alive: to manifest Jesus to the world.

When Mary treasured the words of the Lord concerning her life and, ultimately, the life of her Son, she esteemed them too much to abuse them through improper use. I doubt very much that she fully understood what the angel was saying to her when he announced that she would conceive the Messiah by the Holy Spirit. Again, this is often one of the ways we know God has spoken to us: He speaks outside of what we would reason or plan for ourselves. Plus, He often speaks to us in a way that invites us to seek Him more, as well as to depend upon Him for understanding—both for the word itself and for seeing that word fulfilled.

In the Old Testament, when Joseph, the son of Jacob, was a young man, he was known for his dreams. These dreams were of his own significance and brilliant future, promised to him by God. However, he made the mistake of carelessly making these dreams known beyond what was needed. (See Genesis 37:5–11.) It was the equivalent of allowing all the neighborhood children to drink from his expensive glassware. This mistake cost him dearly and possibly delayed the dreams' fulfillment. Mary did not make the same mistake.

It's important to remember that in the kingdom of God, we attract what we treasure, whether it is good news or bad news, testimonies or gossip, friendships or conflicts. In this case, when we value the word of the Lord, His voice, we see an increase in our personal lives. His word (either through Scripture or directly) is one of the most priceless of all treasures.

"By faith we inherit promises." (See Hebrews 11:33.) It is obvious that faith helps to bring about the fulfillment of God's promises. When we respond in faith to something He has spoken to us, the answer to that promise is imminent. But whenever I read verse 33 of Hebrews 11, the great chapter on faith, I wonder if perhaps the writer is telling us not that faith brings about answers to promises but that faith attracts the promises themselves. I've watched this happen for years. Those who live in a high level of "abiding faith" often hear and receive promises from God that others miss. God is a good steward, giving promises to those who will show proper care for the word given. I think this is one of the beautiful aspects of the kingdom. In my words, it goes something like this: "By faith, we attract and inherit the actual promises of God themselves. And the faith that attracts the promise also stewards well that word, until it is fulfilled."

It is true that there are times when what God has spoken to us has been predetermined to happen regardless of our direct involvement. We simply *"stand by and see the salvation of the LORD"* (Exodus 14:13 NASB), which He accomplishes on our behalf. Whenever I'm privileged to see this happen for myself or a family member or friend, it is a personal favorite of mine among the ways God works. And yet there are other times where our direct response to God's word is necessary for its fulfillment. It concerns me that when I stand before the Lord, I might see promises that were meant to be fulfilled but didn't come to fruition simply because I waited for Him to act instead of living as a responsible steward of all that God had spoken. It takes wisdom to know the difference between these two kinds of promises. This is a matter of prayer, of asking God for discernment and following His direction in faith.

> ***GOD OFTEN SPEAKS TO US IN A WAY THAT INVITES US TO SEEK HIM MORE, AS WELL AS TO DEPEND UPON HIM FOR UNDERSTANDING—BOTH FOR THE WORD ITSELF AND FOR SEEING THAT WORD FULFILLED.***

ALLOW YOUR HEART TO REST IN GOD

We hear best when our hearts are at rest. But, honestly, my need to hear from God is at its highest level when I am anxious and afraid. Hearing is what brings me to a place of trust and rest. It's what reintroduces me to peace. Therefore, the painful reality is that when I most need a word from God, I'm most likely to miss it due to my anxiety. Thankfully, being aware of this conflict helps because the fix is simple. I didn't say it is *easy*, but it is simple, like most kingdom solutions: acknowledging God's lordship. Our acknowledgment of His lordship fixes most problems.

Feeling bad about our anxious feelings doesn't bring us rest. And mere acknowledgment of wrong thinking doesn't create right thinking. But true repentance does. Repentance is illustrated in two words: *from* and *toward*, as in *"repentance **from** dead works and...faith **toward** God"* (Hebrews 6:1 NKJV, NASB). Again, regretting my anxiety doesn't remove it, but dealing with the cause does. At the root of anxiety and fear is misplaced trust. We need to repent for trusting in anything other than God, whether it is our opinions, resources, experiences, or the ideals, thoughts, and values of others. They all compete for that one place that only God deserves—our God, in whom we trust. Only One is perfectly faithful. Not to trust Him is the essence of foolishness.

Sometimes we miss our opportunity to repent because, as I mentioned above, we think a simple acknowledgment of our error fixes everything. It doesn't. It is godly sorrow that leads us to repentance. (See 2 Corinthians 7:10.) Too many people have sorrow for the pain that their sin has caused in their lives, but not sorrow for the sin itself. The pain of realizing how we've hurt the heart of our Father is the kind of pain that leads us to abandon the sin altogether.

Thus, whenever we find ourselves filled with anxiety or fear and unable to hear God's voice, we have several tools to help us begin hearing again. The first is to quiet our hearts into a place of rest and trust in God's sovereignty in our lives. As we confess our lack of trust, we should also confess all known sin, as this is an obvious place to restore our relationship with God. Confession draws the great Forgiver into our situation. We should also worship the Lord, because worship is an intimate expression of affection and adoration toward God. Another tool is to meditate on God's Word. His Word reveals His mind. Whenever we meditate on the Word, the Author shows up, helping to establish His heart in ours. Additionally, it is critical for us to learn to confess and declare all that God has promised us in His Word. Aligning our response to our situations with His mind and thoughts will bring breakthrough, often enabling us to play a responsible part in seeing the fulfillment of His promises.

RECEIVE GOD'S WORD EVEN WHEN IT SEEMS PERPLEXING

Since Jesus is the Word of God, and He is everywhere, His voice is always present. This statement, of course, is an apparent contradiction to what I said earlier in this chapter about God being silent at times. We must understand that there is the overt voice of God and there is the covert voice of God. The overt voice of God is specific to a need or question. It is much more obvious and outward, and it is not very easy to miss if you're looking and listening for it. The covert voice of God is manifested in His presence rather than in concepts or specifics. When we understand this, we learn how to maintain abiding faith when things don't seem to make sense or give us the clarity we are crying out for. Recognizing the difference between these two aspects of God's voice is critical to helping us grow in challenging times.

For me, one of the most fascinating stories in the entire Bible is the account in John 6 of the multiplication of the loaves and fish, as well as what occurred afterward. The crowd that had gathered to hear Jesus that day was massive, so thousands upon thousands of people were present to partake of this provision. There's little doubt that other miracles were also in abundance there, as performing miracles was an everyday occurrence for Jesus. Yet the crowds were gathered not only to see the miracles but also to hear Jesus speak, because no one had ever spoken the way He did. Over and over again, whenever He spoke, the crowds were stunned at His teaching.

But the following day, most people's attitude toward Jesus and His teaching shifted. Jesus began to explain that the only way to be one of His disciples was to "eat His flesh and drink His blood." If there ever was a people who rejected any hint of cannibalism, it was the Jews. As you read through John 6, you note the outrage from the crowd when they hear Jesus's words. It seems that every time you see people arguing over His words, He turns up the intensity. What an interesting and painful lesson in leadership it is to see how little effort Jesus put into explaining His message to calm their fears. The Twelve no doubt wanted Jesus to offer an explanation to the crowd, as they likely loved Jesus's (and their) newfound popularity with the people. And now they saw the crowds leaving in disgust. The Scriptures even record that some of His most committed followers left that day. (See verse 66.) They couldn't handle the conflict of ideas in their minds, the God-given mystery.

It's apparent that all of us need to face the tension found in mystery. Even Jesus's proven disciples needed this challenge. God is a Father who rewards those who seek Him. And there are no rewards where there are no choices to be made. Jesus already knew who wouldn't respond well to this challenge and who would respond well (responding to mystery with abiding faith). He knew who would not believe and who would believe. Faith is the intended outcome of His voice. Always. *"Faith comes by hearing"* (Romans 10:17 NKJV). Jesus is trustworthy, a truth we proclaim in every act of faith toward Him—even abiding faith in the midst of mystery.

But what moves me most about this story is Jesus's comment about His words—more specifically, the confusing teaching that seemed to hint at cannibalism. Jesus said, *"The words that I have spoken to you are spirit and are life"* (John 6:63 NASB). He is the Word made flesh, yet when He speaks, His words become *"spirit."* When Jesus challenged the Twelve, asking if they, too, were planning to leave Him, Peter answered, *"Lord, to whom shall we go? You have words of eternal life"* (John 6:68 NASB). Peter is often used as an example of what not to do because he was often impulsive and spoke foolishly. But he also gets it right a lot, too, as he did in this response. Let me take some liberty in briefly explaining what I believe Peter's answer meant to him, because I don't think he understood the spiritual mystery better than the crowds who left did. To me, Peter is saying, "We don't understand Your teaching any more than the crowds who left do. But what we do know is that, every time You speak, we find out why we're alive. Your words introduce us to life. Even the words we don't understand. So, no, we're not leaving."

Peter's mind may have been baffled by Jesus's teachings, but he knew in his spirit that he was hearing words of life. The same is true for each of us. We know in our spirits when we hear the voice of the Holy Spirit, who is always speaking to us and whose impact on us is immeasurable—and we know that it is life to us.

8

GOD-BIRTHED DREAMS, CREATIVE EXPRESSIONS, AND FULFILLED DESIRES

Learning to hear the voice of God is vital because we are on the brink of creative expressions through the church that the world has never seen before. But these creative expressions are completely dependent upon our surrender to and relationship with the Holy Spirit, and then receiving and carrying out His vision as He works through us.

CREATIVITY AND THE HOLY SPIRIT

The Holy Spirit played a remarkable role in the creation of all things: *"In the beginning...the Spirit of God was hovering over the face of the waters"* (Genesis 1:1–2 NKJV). This imagery is likened to a mother hen who broods over her eggs. In doing so, she creates the ideal atmosphere for her chicks to hatch and thrive. Likewise, the Holy Spirit broods over many things in our lives, always producing the atmosphere necessary for a full expression of life-giving creativity. Being endowed with this creativity is a normal result of spending time in God's manifest presence.

This reality gives us brilliant insight into the nature and birthplace of creativity in the life of a believer. Being sons and daughters of the Creator affords us unique access to His gifts, callings, and anointings.

DESIGNED TO CREATE AND INNOVATE

We were made and redeemed for a creative partnership with the Father through His Spirit. Our creativity is directed through the God-given dreams and desires we have for our lives. Such dreams and desires are formed through countless influences, including our upbringing, relatives, friends, and experiences. All of these aspects are tools that, when guided and empowered by the Holy Spirit, can help to shape us into the creatives God always intended us to be.

In the Old Testament, under the leadership of Moses, a tabernacle was built to serve the children of Israel as their "house of God" while they lived in the wilderness. God was very detailed in His design of the tabernacle, specifying the colors, fabrics, building materials, and quality of work the Israelites were to use. This tabernacle was to be unlike anything the Israelites had built previously because it was to house the presence of God Himself.

The work required for this building project was beyond natural human ability. Perhaps it could best be described in this way: human talent was necessary, but the supernatural influence on the human element was even more important. For me, this is the perfect description of the life of a believer in our times. We must offer to God all we are capable of doing, knowing that we need Him to add His immeasurable touch to everything we do.

In the story of the building of the tabernacle, enter a man named Bezalel. He is the first person the Bible mentions as being filled with the Holy Spirit of God. That is remarkable. I would have thought Moses or one of Israel's kings or prophets would have had that honor. Instead, it was an artist, a craftsman. God said of him:

> *And I have filled him with the Spirit of God, in wisdom, in understanding, in knowledge, and in all manner of workmanship, to design artistic works, to work in gold, in silver, in bronze, in cutting jewels for setting, in carving wood, and to work in all manner of workmanship.*
> (Exodus 31:3–5 NKJV)

This creative genius needed the Holy Spirit to be able to create at a level required for this assignment. And if that measure of anointing was available under an inferior covenant, then how much more should we expect God to give it to us under the better covenant established by the blood of Jesus? Being filled with the Holy Spirit was rare in the Old Testament but has become common among believers since the outpouring of the Spirit at Pentecost. (See Acts 2.) When we are filled with the Spirit, we should experience an overall redemptive touch on our ability to love and serve the world around us well as we share creative solutions to the problems we face. Instead of desiring to be rescued out of the hell of this world's present chaos, perhaps we should stand more assertively in our place as creatives, knowing that God has provided solutions and invited us to pursue Him for them. This too is the work of the Holy Spirit.

After all, as noted earlier, *"it is the glory of God to conceal a matter, but the glory of kings is to search out a matter"* (Proverbs 25:2 NKJV, NASB). Jesus said that it is the Father's good pleasure to give us the mysteries of the kingdom. (See Luke 12:32.) Additionally, we are called *"kings and priests to our God"* (Revelation 5:10 NKJV). As I expressed in the previous chapter, our place of royalty is never more clearly seen than when we pursue the mysteries God has hidden for us. Kings and queens understand that it has been given to them to pursue the hidden things. Perhaps this is the secret to John 15:7 (NKJV): *"If you abide in Me, and My words abide in you, you will ask what you desire, and it will shall be done for you."* The outcome of this amazing promise is that we fulfill our role of being co-laborers with God Himself, who responds with answers to our prayers.

Creativity tends to increase in the lives of those who find a problem to solve. It's not just about writing the next novel or painting a picture. While those types of artistic expressions are included, I am speaking more generally of the redemptive plan of God being worked into our lives so that we are moved by the condition of humanity and endeavor to solve its problems through innovation. New technologies, medical breakthroughs, inventions, and other solutions, as well as the kinds of things that add culture and beauty to our lives, all flow from a place of God-given creativity. And, according to the Scriptures, that place is best found in and through the presence of the Spirit of God.

Living in the felt realization of God's presence is the first step to entering into our inherent design, purpose, and promise. While all of God's wonders, works, and plans speak of His greatness, I am especially captivated by His presence because it is from His presence that we discover His nature. The second step is an intentional embracing of all that God says to us, whether through Scripture or directly by His inspiration. His abiding presence, along with the seed of the Word of God, which contains the full expression of His nature, work in us to bring about the fulfillment of the design and purpose that originated in God's heart for us long before anything was made that has been made.

It is essential to learn to recognize God's presence and live in the environment that is natural to all who abide in that presence. The influence of His Spirit on an individual is evidenced through the simple outcome called "freedom." As the Scriptures say, *"Where the Spirit of the Lord is, there is freedom"* (2 Corinthians 3:17 NIV). Some people say this verse might be read like this: "Where the Holy Spirit manifests the lordship of Jesus, freedom is the result."

> *WE WERE CREATED AND REDEEMED FOR A CREATIVE PARTNERSHIP WITH GOD THROUGH HIS SPIRIT.*

GIVING BIRTH TO CREATIVE EXPRESSION

LIVE IN GOD'S REDEMPTION AND GLORY

The apostle Paul addressed humanity's fallen nature when he stated, *"All have sinned and fall short of the glory of God"* (Romans 3:23, various translations). Jesus came to redeem us from the curse of sin. To redeem means "to buy back." The entire human race sold themselves to sin, but Jesus became both Redeemer and redemption's price. The Redeemer bought us back with Himself as the payment. That is extreme love!

Human beings were born to release inspired expressions of creativity, but sin caused us to fall short of the target made for us: God's glory. Even the word *target* doesn't really indicate God's intent. It would be better to say that the glory of God was not merely a target to be hit but was to become our home or dwelling place. Since the glory of God is unending, it is also our ever-increasing destiny. The realm of His glory is that for which we were designed. There is to be an uninterrupted connection between us and God's glorious presence, the place where creativity is inherent.

Fear, anxiety, and worry—results of our fallen nature—often fill the "womb" of our heart, which was originally designed to generate creative expression. When this happens, it blocks our creativity. Unconfessed sin has the same effect of killing our potential. It fills the place designed to creatively release our understanding of the nature of God. The enemy fears the fulfilled dreams and desires of a sanctified people. These manifested dreams and desires illustrate our *reason for being.* Jesus taught that we are to *"let* [our] *light shine before men in such a way"* that people see our good works but *"glorify* [our] *Father who is in heaven"* (Matthew 5:16 NASB). What flows from us is ultimately to bring God glory.

When Jesus took our place of punishment in His suffering and death on the cross, atoning for our sin, we were restored. But restored to what? At a minimum, we are reinstated to our purpose of living in God's glory! Everything that is created has a location or realm in which it is to live. Fish can only survive in the waters God created. Trees and plants can only live in the soil they were made for. And humankind can only live in the realm of God's presence: His rule. His glory. Everything else is spiritual death.

Illustrations and examples of restoration in the Bible are key to helping us understand the wonder of Christ's work of restoration for us. Consider the example of Job. He lost everything, but when God restored him, he regained double of all that he had lost. (See Job 42:10.) And then there's the temple of Solomon that was destroyed. When the temple was rebuilt after the exile and then expanded in the first century, the area of the Temple Mount was twice the area of the original. The picture of restoration is consistent throughout Scripture: God restores to a place greater than before destruction or loss. *"The glory of this latter house shall be greater than of the former"* (Haggai 2:9 KJV).

Jesus restores us to a place greater than where we were before the fall. Consider the case of Jesus's disciples: they left everything to follow Him, but He promised to restore to them a hundred times what they had lost or left behind. (See Mark 10:28–30.) Since this is the case, doesn't it stand to reason that our salvation has restored us to the place of living in the glory of God? And I don't mean when we get to heaven. That's a given. The beauty of our salvation and the wonder of our design is to be seen in the *here and now*. They are to define our lives as believers, true disciples of Jesus Christ. Thus, to live in the glory of God is to live in the manifest presence of Jesus. This, too, is a work of the Spirit of God.

PURSUE GOD-GIVEN DREAMS AND DESIRES

If we think the Holy Spirit is with us to fulfill all of our own dreams and purposes in life, we will live in constant frustration. But when we realize that we are alive to fulfill His dreams, we will live in constant amazement. A side benefit is that in this process of living in our purpose as co-laborers with God, we discover the fulfillment of our dreams beyond what we would normally have natural access to, beyond our intelligence or faith.

God sometimes withholds our ability to see what is right in front of us. He does this for our safety, especially because human beings have an inbuilt desire to create forms, or formulas, according to what we've seen. For example, the Israelites saw a cloud hovering over the tabernacle in the wilderness. God did not reveal any specific form of Himself there but gave a revelation of His face in the cloud, through which He spoke to the Israelites "face to face":[10]

> So watch yourselves carefully, since you *did not see any form* on the day the LORD spoke to you at Horeb from the midst of the fire, *so that you do not act corruptly and make a graven image for yourselves* in the form of any figure.
>
> —Deuteronomy 4:15–16, emphasis added

> The LORD spoke to you *face to face* at the mountain from the midst of the fire. —Deuteronomy 5:4, emphasis added

> These words the LORD spoke to all your assembly at the mountain *from the midst of the fire, of the cloud* and of the thick gloom, with a great voice. —Deuteronomy 5:22, emphasis added[11]

Because the Israelites had a bent toward making idols, God withheld clarity of sight, knowing they would fashion an idol according to what they had seen. While few people would admit to this bent, it becomes evident every time we want to take a shortcut to know His will instead of going through the process of discovering His heart in a matter. The latter takes time—time that we don't always want to spend. When we create formulas, this sometimes removes God's moment-by-moment influence from our lives. As I wrote earlier, formulas take on a *form* that replaces our need for interaction with the Lord. But clarity of sight and creativity are given

10. Bill Johnson, *Face to Face with God*, rev. ed. (Lake Mary, FL: Charisma House, 2015), 88.
11. Johnson, *Face to Face with God*, 88.

to those who embrace a relational journey to know God and make Him known.

The Holy Spirit's role as Teacher especially supports us in the realm of such pursuits because He helps us to discover whether our desires are born of God the Father. Having this assistance is much more critical than we might think. We can easily look at past and present occurrences in the church and see the disasters in the lives of people who chose sin, calling it the will of God. Some of them chose moral failure while calling evil good and good evil. (See Isaiah 5:20.) Still others chose lifestyles that were contrary to the will and purpose of God, often making gods out of their possessions, relationships, jobs, or power. Being tender toward the Holy Spirit and surrendering to Him make our lives a joyful journey, not a fearful one. But resisting Him leads to disasters of all kinds.

There's no question that choosing to live in willful sin or an idolatrous lifestyle have created tragedy after tragedy in people's lives. And yet I have found that there's another error people make that goes almost unnoticed. In fact, it is often treated as the virtue of humility: the failure to dream and take risks. We know that our desires can be evil. But as I described above, our desires, applied appropriately, can actually reveal God to others. Some people try to settle the issue of whether they have heard God's voice or merely their own desires by canceling out any personal desire whatsoever. And while that keeps them from the deception of self-will, it doesn't keep them from the deception that causes them to fail to enter the fullness of their personal design. It can seem strange to us that this fullness involves the expression of our own desires, as influenced by the Holy Spirit. Most believers are so afraid of getting the realm of personal desires wrong that they do little to nothing, not realizing that, by embracing this approach, they are still failing to get it right. And although sin, or falling short of the mark, is always to be zealously avoided, having godly desires that push us to take risks and to pray bold prayers is the other side of the coin. When we move forward in this way and see God act, we reveal Him as a perfect Father who loves us and works through us.

Therefore, while it is a great error to violate the sovereignty of God, it is a great deception to ignore the fact that God has written our role and influence into His sovereign plan. The danger is far beyond theological because what we believe affects how we behave. And to not see our role—or, better yet, our responsibility—is to automatically fall into the trap of assuming that whatever happens in our lives is the will of God. This mindset has caused more anemic Christianity than perhaps any other theological failure to understand "how we do life as believers."

The topic of the role God plays and the role we play is one in which I seem to be most misunderstood. So, in light of my respect for my friends who disagree with me, let me make an extra effort to encourage you to take what I say here with caution and biblical reasoning. Let's try to come to a place of understanding, knowing we serve One who is sovereign. God is in no way controlled or directed by us. And yet this wonderful Father has invited us into a place with Him where we pray, we worship, and we fellowship with Him. This results in our seeing things happen around us that wouldn't have happened without our involvement. It is the beauty of living responsibly before the God who commissions us to do His works.

My reasoning goes like this: God has not designed us to be robots or computers that produce programmed outcomes. On the contrary, we are living, willing co-laborers with the sovereign One who has invited us into places of influence with Him. He invites us to "come and reason together." (See Isaiah 1:18.) I possess no intelligence that He needs, no insights He doesn't already have, and no gifting that did not originate with Him in the first place. All I have to offer Him is my uniqueness as a created being who is a worshipper by choice. In my uniqueness, I offer my will, obedience, and adoration as an offering. Daily. I have no doubt that I see only a very small measure of why He would want to co-labor with me. In my commitment to efficiency and excellence, *I* wouldn't have chosen me! At all. But as a dad, I would choose any one of my children for any task. God is a Father. Therein lies the secret behind His plan that we co-labor with Christ: it is because He is our heavenly Father.

I should probably add that I have no desire to change God's mind. I love His will and really don't want to have my own way. Having our own way turns out disastrously, and the same result may be seen on the pages of Scripture. And yet there is something beautiful and deeply mysterious about a God who, as a perfect Father, wants us to influence Him. God made sure it is recorded in Scripture that He has at times changed what He has said He would do as a result of people's supplications. (See, for example, Jonah 3.)

> *THERE IS SOMETHING BEAUTIFUL AND DEEPLY MYSTERIOUS ABOUT A GOD WHO, AS A PERFECT FATHER, WANTS US TO INFLUENCE HIM.*

OUR CREATIVE PURPOSE: FRIENDSHIP WITH GOD

It's normal to long to have a place in the Father's eyes where what we think and say matters to Him. It's not a desire to control Him or to have our own way. In my experience, it's quite the opposite because it expresses something that is already in the heart of God for us. Perhaps Jesus's statement, *"No longer do I call you servants…; but I have called you friends, for all things that I heard from My Father I have made known to you"* (John 15:15 NKJV) is actually all about that. Servants are task-oriented. Their primary concern is to complete what is on the to-do list from the master, but a friend has a completely different perspective. Their concern is with the *heart* behind the to-do list. They are invested in the mood, desires, and well-being of their friend. Similarly, I always want to do God's will. But my relationship with Him is what makes His to-do list an invitation to partnership with Him that is beyond a mere command.

I'm not a friend of God merely because I sing a praise song about being His friend. True friendship takes time and is granted to those who have proven to be faithful, those who have shown they are trustworthy. And if I understand that He considers me to be His friend, I have a responsibility to both receive from Him and give to Him to solidify and illustrate that relationship.

I receive from God's friendship because He transforms me daily into the image of His Son, Jesus the Christ. And everything He says and does in my life is to be evidenced in the Christlikeness seen in me. I am equally responsible to give. Regardless of how qualified or unqualified I feel, I must respond to His invitation. And while this language may seem a bit strong, please understand it in this context: we must "put a demand" on our friendship with God. Again, this must not be seen as an effort to control Him. But there needs to be intentionality in our effort to fulfill all that was in God's heart when He invited us into that position of friendship. And as uncomfortable as this subject makes me feel, it was the Father Himself who at least one time commanded us to *"command"* Him: *"Ask Me of things to come concerning My sons; and concerning the work of My hands, you command Me"* (Isaiah 45:11 NKJV). This could be one of the harder challenges we face in our test to walk in obedience.

I mentioned earlier that this whole journey of the life of a believer is about discovering and revealing our perfect heavenly Father to a planet of orphans—those who still need to be reconciled to the Father. Is that not what Jesus commissioned us to do? The overwhelming theme of the gospel of John is that Jesus came to earth to reveal the Father. He revealed the Father not only through His life, but also through His death and resurrection. Jesus said to those who followed Him, *"As the Father has sent Me, I also send you"* (John 20:21 NKJV, NASB). The implication is that, at least in part, we too are to reveal our Father. Let us seek to do this by remaining filled with the Holy Spirit, seeking His thoughts, committing our God-given desires to Him, and allowing the Spirit to flow through us in life-changing creative and innovative expressions that meet the needs of others.

PRAYERS OF PURPOSE AND FULFILLED DESIRES

Earlier, we talked about how the Holy Spirit, as our Helper, intercedes for us and enables us to express our needs and wants to God. Let's now see how we can be transformed, *through our prayers,* to align with God's heart so we can reveal the Father to the world.

Prayer has two primary purposes: prayer changes *circumstances,* and prayer changes *the one who prays.* And it's the latter that is the greater miracle. We are invited to pray as a way of having fellowship with God and being changed, as well as to see His hand move in the issues we face in our lives, the lives of our family members, and in our surroundings—local, national, and international. For me, prayers of fellowship are usually expressions of worship and adoration. When my heart of affection burns for God, I know I'm alive and connected to Him. But prayers of purpose are different in that they find their fulfillment in answers. Outcomes. Changes.

CHANGED THROUGH PRAYER

A series of mini-stories involving the disciples and Jesus found in Luke 9 beautifully illustrates how we can be transformed in prayer so we can receive answers to prayer. We see how the disciples' requests of Jesus became opportunities to change their perspective. In these stories, the Twelve made request after request that the Master rejected in the form in which they asked it. But it's the process of their coming to understand Jesus's will that moves me most.

Here's the setting: The disciples had just returned from their mission trip, during which they were to preach the gospel of the kingdom, heal the sick, raise the dead, cast out demons, and cleanse lepers. Jesus sent them to their hometowns in pairs. (See Luke 9:1–6; see also Matthew 10:1–15; Mark 6:7–13.) Afterward, they regrouped with a profound sense of success because they had seen the same things happen in their outreaches that they had witnessed Jesus do daily. It is in this context that we see the first problem arise. The disciples developed an inflated sense of personal significance. We note in Luke 9:46 that they argued as to which of them was the greatest. They seemed to think that the ways in which God used them in ministry was a sign of His approval of *all* their thoughts, ambitions, and character. The same mistake has been made through the ages by those who, after an act of sin or compromise in thought or behavior, saw that

God used them as powerfully as before. What many people fail to realize is that when God moves powerfully, it's a validation of His Word, not always of the character of the servant of the Lord. We see the disciples' mistaken self-perceptions that were prompted by the answers to prayer they received during their mission trip. Again, these perceptions were no doubt shaped by their fruitfulness in ministry, perceptions that would easily be driven by competition through comparison. Comparison is the deadly practice of so many.

In this situation, we see one of the most remarkable things about Jesus that we often miss: He didn't rebuke His disciples for their desire for greatness; instead, He taught them what it truly means to be great. (See verses 47–48.) It's hard to spend time with Jesus—feeding on His words, seeing what only He can do and the actions of service He demonstrated—and not hunger for more. *Desire* is a sign that we're alive. Although this conversation in which Jesus taught His disciples about true greatness may not seem like an example of their being challenged to change through prayer, let me remind you that Jesus is the eternal Son of God, with whom the disciples had the opportunity to speak directly about many matters, and all conversation with Him is prayer.

The disciples weren't scolded or punished because they had dreams or desires. As we saw earlier, the key is that, although we are invited to pursue our desires, we must remain loyal to Jesus, expecting Him to prune anything and everything in our lives that is contrary to His purpose for us. However, let us also remember that many people desire nothing and call it discipleship. Their fear of getting it wrong is greater than their fear of not getting it right. Most of us have heard the saying "It's easier to steer a car that is moving." Many people stand still, waiting for direction, instead of following their heart, knowing that God will steer the car as it moves. It's actually an issue of trust. Do we believe God is big enough to direct our hearts even when we're not in a place of deep prayer?

Right after Jesus taught His disciples the meaning of true greatness, another mini-story emerges: John lets Jesus know the disciples found someone casting out demons in Jesus's name, but this person wasn't in their group, so they tried to stop him from doing this. (See verse 49.) There's little doubt John expected to be congratulated for protecting the integrity of their group and not allowing others to contaminate or dilute what Jesus was teaching them. Jesus's response was unexpected by all: *"Do not forbid him, for he who is not against us is on our side"* (verse 9:50 NKJV). Jesus encouraged the disciples to broaden their view of who belonged to "their group." It was the same message He had taught them earlier: *"My mother and My brothers are these who hear the word of God and do it"* (Luke 8:21 NKJV, NASB).

THE CONDITIONS OF PRAYER

In these mini-stories, we see how Jesus replied to the disciples' requests and statements in a manner they didn't expect. They imagined that one of them would be selected by Jesus to be greatest in the kingdom, and they thought Jesus would agree with them that an "outsider" not be allowed to minister the way they had been doing as part of Jesus's group. In light of Jesus's redirection of these expectations, I realize that some people might remind me that *no* is an answer we may receive from God. I acknowledge that here and now. This is important to understand, especially as a process of discovering that we just prayed something that wasn't the will of God. Again, unfortunately, there have been many unanswered prayers that *were* the will of God, but the conditions for the prayer itself were not met. It wasn't that God said an outright no.

Case in point: A father brought his demonized son to the disciples for healing and deliverance. They tried and failed to deliver the son. In other words, their prayers for this child were not answered. When the father saw Jesus coming, he brought his son to Him. Jesus performed the miracle that was needed. (See, for example, Matthew 17:14–21.) So, what was God's will? Healing and deliverance, of course. But it didn't happen as a result of the best efforts of the disciples. When they don't seem to receive an answer to their prayers, most people stop at that point, assuming it wasn't God's time for the healing or deliverance to occur. The explanations that allow for this behavior are nauseating. And I've given them, too, to relieve myself of the pressure of not getting an answer: "God has perfect timing for everything. We must trust Him to bring about the desired answer in His time." That statement is 100 percent true. And yet it is only one example of the excuses we resort to instead of learning to contend for the answer that reveals the will of God. And what is His will? "*On earth as it is in heaven*" (Matthew 6:10 NKJV, NASB). What is His will? "*Now is the day of salvation*" (2 Corinthians 6:2). The word *salvation* carries in its meaning healing, deliverance, and the forgiveness of sin.[12] When is it the will of God to heal, deliver, and forgive? *Today.* Today is the day.

The disciples took Jesus aside and asked Him why they weren't able to bring about the boy's deliverance. He told them, "*This kind does not go out except by prayer and fasting*" (Matthew 17:21, various translations). Yet, as far as we know, Jesus had neither fasted nor prayed specifically about this need. We tend to pray and fast for particular needs, and this is certainly a legitimate practice. But Jesus seemed to have had a *lifestyle* of prayer and fasting that was not restricted to a particular circumstance.

While Jesus's instruction about prayer and fasting is vital, I think the key to the story is that when the disciples didn't get an answer to their prayer, they took Jesus aside to find out why. They didn't assume their lack of a breakthrough was the will of God, as that perspective was never modeled by Jesus Himself. So much of what we teach or accept as the will of God cannot be found in the lifestyle of Jesus. It's easier to blame God's sovereignty than it is to pursue Him and, in the process, become the person necessary to see continual breakthroughs of this nature.

Thankfully, Jesus came along and brought the needed freedom to that child; otherwise, we might have found the disciples creating a theology that allowed for the absence of a breakthrough.

TESTED AND QUALIFIED

How can we persevere in our faith and hope when we're in the midst of situations where we don't receive answers to our prayers, or our dreams

12. *Strong's*, G4982, Blue Letter Bible Lexicon, https://www.blueletterbible.org/lexicon/g4982/kjv/tr/0-1/.

aren't fulfilled, as soon as we expected? For me, God often sets up a series of tests that will ultimately qualify me for the fulfillment of my biggest prayers. Let me insert here that in no way do we ever *earn* answers to prayer. They always come as a gift of grace. And yet there are conditions in our lives that can disqualify us from the answer we have asked for. Perhaps a better way to say this is that if God answered the prayer we just prayed, the answer might destroy us. For example, I don't think any of us could live under the pressure that would come with the immediate answer to the prayer "God, heal everyone I pray for!" We would be front-page news around the world in a matter of days, and the social, economic, mental, and relational pressure would destroy the best of us. And so, God works on us, qualifying us for greater and greater measures of what we have just prayed for.

Joseph in the Old Testament is a great example of this. We see in Psalm 105:19 (NKJV) that *"until the time that his* [Joseph's] *word came to pass, the word of the LORD tested him."* That is an extraordinary statement. We know that Joseph shared with his family his dreams of ruling over them, but this message wasn't well-received. In fact, his brothers wanted to kill him, but they ultimately sold him into slavery instead. Joseph went through a series of challenges that would strip him of everything that would hinder his role as a leader who would eventually be the salvation of his entire family, as well as of the Israelites as a nation. (See Genesis 37, 39–47.) We resist being reduced in any way, but this is often the key to our breakthroughs because we are reduced to our real position of strength—one of complete reliance on God to carry out His purposes. That position is one He can build on.

I have always considered that Joseph's dreams, and the way he told them, were 100 percent from the Lord. And I will admit even now that I don't know what was from him and what was from God. But there was something about what Joseph said about his future that he—not God—was responsible for. I believe that is why the psalmist declares, *"Until the time that* [Joseph's] *word came to pass...."* And whether it was Joseph's prophetic word about his destiny or about the individuals he served in prison, the word of the Lord tested him to shape and qualify him for the fulfillment of his own prophecy. The word of the heavenly Father worked on Joseph until he became a man who could correctly and honorably steward his own destiny. This gives us a significant insight into how the Holy Spirit helps us to align our desires with God's and realize our dreams. As I described earlier, the Spirit continuously works to conform us into the image of Jesus so we can be shaped and qualified to carry out those dreams.

> ***WE RESIST BEING REDUCED IN ANY WAY, BUT THIS IS OFTEN THE KEY TO OUR BREAKTHROUGHS BECAUSE WE ARE REDUCED TO OUR REAL POSITION OF STRENGTH—ONE OF COMPLETE RELIANCE ON GOD TO CARRY OUT HIS PURPOSES.***

We often pray great prayers. Big prayers. My conviction is that when we do so, the Holy Spirit immediately begins to work on us, making us into someone who can survive and thrive under the weightiness of the answer. The glory of God upon a person either exposes cracks in that person's foundation (for the purpose of mending them) or establishes the individual in a way that they are absolutely committed to having God receive all the glory.

All of this seems to be connected to this familiar verse from Proverbs 13:12 (NASB): *"Hope deferred makes the heart sick, but desire fulfilled is a tree of life."* Solomon wrote that having fulfilled desires connects us to a *"tree of life."* And Jesus said that fulfilled desires give us fullness of joy. (See John 16:24.) These are two sides of the same coin because we were designed to have desires and then to see those desires fulfilled by a loving Father, reinforcing our identity in Him and giving us abundant life, measured by joy.

Because we were designed for such a heavenly partnership, it is affirming whenever we see our God-birthed desires answered and fulfilled. As described earlier, it is the Holy Spirit who helps us discern whether our desires are born of God or whether we are trying to use Scripture to persuade Him to let us have our own way. We all need the help of the Holy Spirit during this journey because the full effect of God's purpose for our lives will have such a significant impact on us and the world around us. This area of fulfilled desire is a major threat to the enemy's influence on the earth and is therefore a chief target of his. In the answers to our prayers, our heavenly Father is revealed as a loving Father. We owe that revelation of God to the world, so we must pray to receive answers for ourselves and others.

Fulfilled desires have another benefit that I've only recently recognized: they add days to our lives and strength to our days. *"Who satisfies your years with good things, so that your youth is renewed like the eagle"* (Psalm 103:5 NASB). There's something medicinal about fulfilled desires and dreams—answers to prayer. Our realization that we have received God's favor, along with our increased sense of identity and purpose, serves to bring more strength and even years to our lives. We've all seen those who die soon after losing their reason for living. The opposite is also true: strength and increase of days come to those who delight in the benefit of fulfilled God-dreams. The great joy of being used by God is surpassed only by His manifest presence itself.

9

FRUIT, GIFTS, AND THE "MUNDANE"

It would be impossible to make a complete list of the effects of the Holy Spirit upon one life, let alone upon the entire body of Christ. Yet the Scriptures give us stories and lists that reveal the Spirit's nature and power. None of these stories and lists contain Him, in the sense of establishing limits or boundaries on who He is and what He does. But they do reveal essential qualities and aspects of His person and works.

My personal favorite description of the Holy Spirit's work in and through someone is found in the story of Gideon in Judges 6:34. Some Bible translations state that the Spirit of God came "on" or "upon" Gideon. But the wording in the original Hebrew seems dramatically different from this. It states that "the Holy Spirit clothed Himself with Gideon."[13] As my friend Michael Thompson, a great pastor and speaker from Melbourne, Florida, taught many years ago, the Holy Spirit put Gideon on like a glove. This analogy gives a picture of being *possessed by God*.

While I love this Old Testament story of the Holy Spirit working through Gideon, there's no way that Gideon's anointing could have been superior to what God has promised and made available to all who are *filled with the Holy Spirit* under the new covenant. Superior blessings never come from inferior covenants. God takes us "*from glory to glory*" (2 Corinthians 3:18 NKJV, NASB). I mention this truth again for one reason: to emphasize that what is available to us now is greater than what Gideon had—and we must pursue it. That means that the wonder and beauty of Gideon's experience are surpassed in the life of every believer who is truly filled with the Holy Spirit.

ARE WE FILLED?

Sometimes we become so familiar with a truth that we are no longer impressed or even impacted by it. Having the Holy Spirit dwelling in us seems to be one of those realities. Consider this thought: in Ephesians 3:19 (NKJV), Paul says that we are to be "*filled with all the fullness of God.*" I'm not sure that there is a more incomprehensible idea than that one! God is everywhere, all at once. Galaxies are filled with Him. The mere size of the eternal One is immeasurable. And that One wants to fill us *with His fullness*. If He only wanted to fill us with Himself, we'd be the most blessed part of creation. But when it says He wants to do so *with His fullness*? Once again, these are not ideas to comprehend. They are to be embraced with the heart and considered as invitations to a deeper relationship with Him and a greater awareness of our design and purpose. Through surrender to the beauty of such mysteries, let's come under the influence of truths beyond the reach of human intellect or emotional capacity.

Another statement about this fullness is found in Ephesians 5:18 (NKJV): "*Do not be drunk with wine,...but be filled with the Spirit.*" I have

13. *NKJV Spirit-Filled Life Bible* (Nashville, TN: Thomas Nelson, 1991), 357.

heard Randy Clark, the great author, revivalist, and international speaker, brilliantly expound on the meaning of this verse. He reminds us that wine has no effect on a person while it is in a bottle. It still has no effect when it is in a glass. It must get from the glass to the stomach of an individual to have its intoxicating effect. The lesson here is not complicated. When something is in you, it has an effect. *"Be filled with the Spirit"* is not a suggestion. It is a command: live under the "intoxicating" influence of the Holy Spirit.

I heard a story some years ago about a great evangelist who was speaking at a church when one of the elders arrived drunk on wine. The pastor was obviously upset and talked with the evangelist about the discipline he should bring to this man. The guest speaker asked if all the other elders had come filled with the Spirit, as that is the other half of the command against drunkenness. The point is, we are rightfully offended by the intoxication of the elder, but we are rarely offended by leaders who are not filled with the Spirit.

The bottom line is that when the Holy Spirit takes up residence in us, all of heaven expects there to be results *in* us (character) and *through* us (in the supernatural and natural gifts we exercise to express Him well). The very presence of God in a person makes the impossibilities of life possible.

FRUIT: CHARACTER TRANSFORMED

The abiding presence of God always has an impact on the thought life, behavior, and character of a person. The fruit, or effects, of the Holy Spirit's working in an individual are measurable. They are the evidence of grace at work in the child of God. One of the major differences between law and grace is that law *requires* while grace *enables*. The indwelling presence of God, through grace, brings about change from the inside out. Religious cultures—in the negative sense of those that embrace form without power, and ritual without relationship—also require change of their members. But such change is always from the outside in. In other words, it's related to what people can accomplish through human effort, discipline, and determination. In those cultures, the incentive to bring about change often comes through group thought or peer pressure. In saying this, I don't want to cast a negative light on personal discipline, which is such an important part of our lives. It's just that self-effort cannot change the nature of a person. Only the grace of God, through the indwelling presence of the Holy Spirit, can bring about a transformational experience. In the kingdom, we are transformed from the inside out, from where the Spirit of God lives, toward the people and circumstances that surround us. This transformation is absolutely necessary because it enables and equips us to represent Jesus well.

The apostle Paul described this effect in his epistle to the church at Galatia:

> *But the fruit of the [Holy] Spirit [the work which His presence within accomplishes] is love, joy (gladness), peace, patience (an even temper, forbearance), kindness, goodness (benevolence), faithfulness, gentleness (meekness, humility), self-control (self-restraint, continence). Against such things there is no law [that can bring a charge]. And those who belong to Christ Jesus (the Messiah) have crucified the flesh (the godless human nature) with its passions and appetites and desires. If we live by the [Holy] Spirit, let us also walk by the Spirit. [If by the Holy Spirit we have our life in God, let us go forward walking in line, our conduct controlled by the Spirit.] Let us not become vainglorious and self-conceited, competitive and challenging and provoking and irritating to one another, envying and being jealous of one another.*
>
> (Galatians 5:22–26 AMPC)

The first thing to note about this passage is that when all these virtues are listed—*love, joy, peace, patience, kindness, goodness, faithfulness, gentleness,* and *self-control*—they are mentioned as only one fruit. Singular. They are not called the "fruits" of the Holy Spirit. That amazes me in so many ways. It's also extremely encouraging to see that whenever God is dealing with us in a specific area, His transforming work will touch every area of our lives, all at the same time. In other words, He's not just trying to make me more patient, but He is trying to make me kinder or more joyful (or any of the other qualities listed) at the same time. All the virtues are interrelated.

GIFTS: MINISTRY EXPRESSIONS

As we read through the four Gospels, we see Jesus displaying the works and wonders of a loving Father. Let me emphasize again that Jesus said, "If you've seen Me, you've seen the Father." (See John 14:9.) His primary mission was to reveal the Father. And the exercise of the gifts of the Holy Spirit accomplishes this in a variety of ways.

In discussing the gifts of the Holy Spirit, I want to remind you that, although Jesus is eternally God, in His earthly life, He chose to restrict Himself to doing what He saw His Father doing and saying what He heard His Father saying. In Acts 10:38 (NKJV, NASB), Jesus is described as *"healing all who were oppressed by the devil,* ***for God was with Him****."* As we have discussed, this verse is not saying Jesus isn't God Himself. Instead, it is emphasizing an all-important aspect of the gospel: Jesus became a man and set an example that we could follow *if the same Holy Spirit is involved.* The works and miracles of Jesus are too numerous to fully record in detail. (See John 21:25.) But everywhere we see Jesus at work, we see the Holy Spirit at work. As God, Jesus could do anything at any time. But His lifestyle was one of absolute dependency on the Father, and it became the model for all who would follow Him.

If Jesus performed His miracles only as God, I am still impressed, but I am only a spectator. When I realize that He performed them as a man dependent on God, I am no longer satisfied to stay the way I am. Even if I feel that I fall short in living this miracle lifestyle well, I just don't have the right to change my assignment to something different or "easier" when Jesus's giving us this model to follow came at such an extreme cost.

The Holy Spirit is the One who took what Jesus was receiving from the Father (what the Father was saying and doing) and brought it into the practical by revealing the Father through Jesus's words and works. Jesus lived dependently upon the Father for everything He said and did. But it was the Holy Spirit, *the dove who remains* (see John 1:32–33), who made the miracle realm common through Jesus's daily life. And He wants to do the same through us.

> *IN THE KINGDOM, WE ARE TRANSFORMED FROM THE INSIDE OUT, FROM WHERE THE SPIRIT OF GOD LIVES, TOWARD THE PEOPLE AND CIRCUMSTANCES THAT SURROUND US.*

MANIFESTATIONS OF THE SPIRIT: BUILDING UP BELIEVERS

The apostle Paul addressed this reality of the Holy Spirit working His gifts through us most clearly to the church at Corinth. The new believers there were accustomed to serving many gods. But through Paul's instruction, they were learning that all the various manifestations of the supernatural came from *the one Spirit*, not from a variety of spirits or gods.

Paul gave the Corinthian believers a list of a number of gifts, or expressions, of the Holy Spirit. As I wrote above, I don't believe this list was to limit or somehow contain the ways in which God works. But it does reveal His ways and His desire to work through every believer through supernatural means.

> *There are varieties of effects, but the same God who works all things in all persons. But to each one is given the manifestation of the Spirit for the common good. For to one is given* ***the word of wisdom*** *through the Spirit, and to another* ***the word of knowledge*** *according to the same Spirit; to another* ***faith*** *by the same Spirit, and to another* ***gifts of healing*** *by the one Spirit, and to another* ***the effecting of miracles,*** *and to another* ***prophecy,*** *and to another* ***the distinguishing of spirits,*** *to another* ***various kinds of tongues,*** *and to another* ***the interpretation of tongues.*** *But one and the same Spirit works all these things, distributing to each one individually just as He wills.*
>
> (1 Corinthians 12:6–11 NASB)

To begin with, it is important for us to recognize three notable ideas from this passage: (1) each of these gifts is called a *"manifestation"* of the Holy Spirit; (2) each is given according to the will of the Holy Spirit; and (3) each is to be used for *"the common good."* All these gifts are for the edification of the believer. Only one gift—praying in tongues—is used for personal edification.

The personal expression of tongues is for prayer and praise, and it builds up the speaker spiritually. This type of tongues does not need to be interpreted because it's not for the edification of the corporate gathering. If you think every tongue needs to be interpreted, then you have missed some of Paul's teachings (see, for example, 1 Corinthians 13:1; 14:4, 27–28), as well as one of the points of the day of Pentecost. Certain people were confused and mocked the 120 as they all spoke with tongues they did not understand. This was the one service where no one knew enough to exhibit control to remove the Holy Spirit's influence.

At least two of my relatives wrote in perfect Chinese after they were baptized in the Holy Spirit. This, of course, was a language they did not know. When a Chinese-speaking missionary came through town, he read these documents and told them that one of them had written praises to God, and the other had quoted the Twenty-Third Psalm. You'll notice that what I just described (writing in an unfamiliar language through the Spirit) is not specifically on Paul's list of gifts given by the Holy Spirit. But it is consistent with the nature of that list—mysteries revealed for the edification of others. It doesn't contradict it but instead adds to our realization of how the gifts of the Spirit work and what they are for.

My opinion is that because the Holy Spirit, the Giver of spiritual gifts, lives in every believer, it is possible for us to function in any of the gifts at any time. They are contained in His person, and He dwells with us.

When we don't seem to exhibit spiritual gifts, part of the problem is that we tend to think these gifts will "come" to us. In other words, that some sort of sovereign act of God will force or drive us into the manifestation of a gift. Consider this: Chapter 12 of 1 Corinthians unveils brilliant teaching about the gifts. Chapter 14 expands on this teaching with more practical instruction. But sandwiched in between these two chapters is one of the most necessary chapters in the entire Bible: 1 Corinthians 13, the chapter on love. Why? Because the gifts are for the edification of the believer. Chapter 14 starts with, "*Pursue love, yet desire earnestly spiritual gifts*" (verse 1 NASB). This implies that gifts don't necessarily come to us automatically. They must be earnestly desired and sought after. And what greater motivation for pursuing these various manifestations of the Holy Spirit could there be than the motivation of love for the church—seeing each person edified and encouraged? The love chapter sets us up to pursue manifestations of the Holy Spirit for the right reason.

Thus, chapter 12 emphasizes that the gifts are given according to the will of the Holy Spirit. Chapter 14 emphasizes that they are given to those who earnestly desire and pursue them. That's not a contradiction. It's an expansion of a mysterious concept that is to help us better understand the partnership between the sovereignty of God and the desire and pursuit of His people. God's sovereignty reigns supreme. As God, He needs nothing from us. But He has written us into His plan, so our passions should mirror His will for us. Perhaps it should be said that we are able to pursue gifts because He first willed for us to live a lifestyle of exercising spiritual gifts, to His glory and the benefit of His people.

Being used by God is not about feeling better about ourselves or our spiritual maturity or significance or importance. The use of spiritual gifts illustrates a commitment to the people of God that says, "Love always seeks the best for others. And how could there be anything better than a supernatural display of God's heart for His people through ongoing manifestations of the Holy Spirit? Therefore, I will passionately pursue manifestations of the Spirit through my life."

It's important to realize that the revelation of the gifts in 1 Corinthians 12 didn't impart the gifts themselves. The list of gifts revealed what we can and must pursue. We often think we understand something because we can quote a principle about it that we've been taught. But a principle is not really understood until it is brought into practical human experience.

NO LONGER MUNDANE

We live in two realities at all times: (1) the natural realm, which is the visible, tangible world in which we live—with its physical laws, principles, and boundaries, and (2) the supernatural realm, or the spiritual world, which is unseen but influences and affects all that we see and hear. While we exist within these two distinct realities, God exists in only one reality: the "supernaturally natural." It's all His. What is supernatural and unexplainable to us is perfectly natural and logical to Him. There is no distinction between the two. Understanding this will help us glean the important truths discussed in the rest of this chapter. We have the opportunity to discover the joy of the supernaturally empowered natural elements of life. Nothing is mundane once God touches it!

Perhaps the best illustration of this reality is found in the life of Solomon. We know Solomon as the man of wisdom. His desire to gain wisdom was first planted in his heart through the instruction of his father, David. (See Proverbs 4:3–9.) When God appeared to Solomon in his sleep and asked him to name whatever he wanted, Solomon chose wisdom. God was so pleased with this choice that he also gave Solomon all the other things (riches, fame, and safety) he might have asked for. (See 1 Kings 3:4–10.)

Soon, Solomon's fame went out all over the known world. People from every nation, sent from all the monarchs of the earth, came to sit at his feet and take in the influence of divine wisdom. (See 1 Kings 4:34.) The most notable visitor was the Queen of Sheba. She spent considerable time with Solomon, asking questions and learning from this great man. After talking with him and seeing the greatness of his royal court, she confessed she had thought that what she'd heard about Solomon was an exaggeration. But she admitted that the half had not been told her. Here's what moves me most about this part of the story: when the Bible, under the Holy Spirit's guidance and inspiration, mentions what stirred the Queen of Sheba about Solomon's wisdom, only mundane things are listed. There's no doubt that Solomon answered mysteries about creation and the meaning of life. I honestly would love to have a record of their conversations. But God chose instead to focus on things like Solomon's house, the food he served, the seating around his table, his servants' clothing, and the stairway from the king's house to the house of God. Stairs, clothing, food, the function of servants, and chairs? Of all the profound things that could have been listed, God chose the everyday. (See 1 Kings 10:1–13.)

I believe that one of our greatest journeys in life is to learn how to yield natural things to God's influence and find His delight in what normally would not seem to be the most exciting parts of our lives. We read in Proverbs, *"In all your ways acknowledge Him, and He will make your paths straight"* (Proverbs 3:6 NASB). *"In all your ways"*: in family relationships, positions of ministry and work, responsibilities, and hobbies—all of it. Recognize God as the source and inspiration in each of those things, and His hand will be released to influence and put a mark on your journey. If and when we involve Him in the simple and practical ways of life, they will receive His touch, and we will find greater meaning for every part of our lives. As for the Queen of Sheba, Scripture says that once she saw all that Solomon had, *"there was no more spirit in her"* (1 Kings 10:5 NKJV, NASB), which basically means she was stunned and speechless. Similarly, people were *"astonished"* whenever Jesus, the Man of wisdom (see 1 Corinthians 1:30), spoke. (See, for example, Matthew 7:28 NKJV.) It's time for the world to become speechless again by witnessing the wisdom and power God wants to flow through us to others.

God truly longs for us to live fully from a place of personal transformation, expressing the gifts and manifestations of the Holy Spirit to further edify and strengthen the people of God, to bring Him glory in all of life. This is our privileged assignment. The two elements of spiritual fruit and gifts give credibility to the gospel. The good news is for all. But it doesn't stop there. It doesn't stop with our becoming people of character or even people of supernatural gifting and power. God also wants to immerse us in His presence in such a way that everything about us is saturated with the God of wonders, the Holy Spirit who dwells in us and among us. Saturated with God on earth, who lives inside of every child of

God. God's desire is to capture and repurpose our natural gifts, assignments, and functions.

> *ONE OF OUR GREATEST JOURNEYS IN LIFE IS TO LEARN HOW TO YIELD NATURAL THINGS TO GOD'S INFLUENCE AND FIND HIS DELIGHT IN WHAT NORMALLY WOULD NOT SEEM TO BE THE MOST EXCITING PARTS OF OUR LIVES.*

REPURPOSED

About five years ago, my wife Beni and I bought a beautiful home, but the style of the interior was dated. We had dreams of something more modern and up-to-date in functionality and beauty. We gutted the house and even removed a couple of the walls. But one of the things I wanted to make sure to do was to repurpose everything originally built into the home that we would not be using there. So, I gave the oak flooring away to a friend, who was able to refinish it and use it in his own home, and it looks wonderful there. The cabinetry in the bathroom was excellent but didn't fit into our design. It now looks amazing in my brother's house. The kitchen cabinets were of the same first-class quality. I had our builder repurpose them by installing them in our garage. I did the same with the sub-zero refrigerator and freezer. My garage is now equipped with excellence and beauty because of the quality of the materials first used in the main house. The top-notch kitchen appliances have found their place in my outdoor kitchen. The point is: I hate waste, but I also wanted a newer feel and function to this beautiful home. Nothing was wasted. Everything was given a new use.

In a similar way, God repurposes every part of our lives. Switching the analogy, every experience and every relationship, good or bad, every past success as well as every failure, goes into the recipe of the Master Chef, who makes *"all things work together for good"* (Romans 8:28 NKJV, KJV). Many of these ingredients have a bitter taste in themselves. But when God redeems them, He repurposes them until they become the gold standard of what He can make out of our lives. This is especially true of our natural gifts. They become repurposed until they give Him place to be revealed in the simplest and most practical ways.

No doubt, the young David worked hard to hone his skills with his sling, but the touch of God on his natural gift took down a giant. (See 1 Samuel 17:40–50.) The mighty men of David trained hard at being excellent soldiers, but their accomplishments, like one man killing eight hundred enemy soldiers with only primitive weapons, were supernatural in effect. (See 2 Samuel 23:8.) I'm sure Peter, James, and John committed themselves to becoming the best fishermen possible so that they might provide for their families, but the time when their boats almost sank because of an abundance of fish (see, for example, Luke 5:1–10) revealed once again that God loves to partner with natural gifts, assignments, and abilities. His touch on the normal changes everything, making all aspects of our lives part of our great adventure with Him.

GOD'S CALLING CARD

In coming chapters, I will talk further about the wonderful subject of being filled with the Spirit. But I want to return to the book of Exodus, which mentions something so mind-boggling about being filled with the Holy Spirit that I must point out again here and now the effects of the Spirit's abiding presence. When He is partnered with, depended upon, and fully yielded to, everything comes into view as a potential object of His purposeful touch.

> *Now the* Lord *spoke to Moses, saying, "See, I have called by name Bezalel, the son of Uri, the son of Hur, of the tribe of Judah. I have filled him with the Spirit of God in* ***wisdom****, in* ***understanding****, in* ***knowledge****, and in* ***all kinds of craftsmanship****, to make* ***artistic designs*** *for work in gold, in silver, and in bronze, and in the cutting of stones for settings, and in the carving of wood, that he may work in all kinds of craftsmanship."* (Exodus 31:1–5 NASB)

This is my favorite example in Scripture of the effects of the Holy Spirit on the natural gifts in our lives. Bezalel was used by God for the building of the intricate furnishings of the tabernacle under Moses's direction. Once more, he is the first person in all of Scripture who is mentioned as being filled with the Holy Spirit. This infilling was manifested in *"wisdom," "understanding," "knowledge," "all kinds of craftsmanship,"* and *"artistic designs."* The effect of wisdom—the initial manifestation of the Spirit's fullness in this man's life—is impressive.

Wisdom is creative in nature, paving the way for an increase in knowledge and understanding. As you can imagine, when these areas are functioning in our lives, they enable us to be influencers in the world in unique and attractive ways. Attractive in the sense that what we bring is valued and desirable by the people we serve. I don't like creating a picture of believers being the only source of solutions for the world's problems. I'm not sure that equation would be good for us. But we must be a primary influence in this way through our heart of love and service for humanity and our "nothing is impossible" approach to the issues of life. The Holy Spirit makes it possible for us to serve well in this way. He has all the answers needed for every issue on the planet. As I wrote in the previous chapter, solutions and creative expressions are waiting to be discovered. Again, the Holy Spirit is so overwhelmingly powerful that it is often easy to forget that He is equally practical.

We often cripple ourselves in this assignment by hoping that we will be rescued from the world's crises instead of being the salt, light, and leaven that the world needs. Each of these elements that Jesus spoke of has an influence on its surroundings. When we look to escape this world to go to heaven, we miss the opportunity to bring heaven to earth in practical ways. Such manifestations of God's kindness, through the work of the Holy Spirit in believers, are His calling card, should onlookers hunger for the Source of such solutions.

If we don't take our rightful place in pursuing answers to the world's needs with excellence, we create a vacuum that unbelievers will often fill. If God's own children won't take advantage of their position to discover solutions (mysteries of the kingdom), God honors anyone who pursues them.

Perhaps He does so in part because of His heart for all humanity, hoping that His kindness will lead people to repentance. (See Romans 2:4.) Let us serve others well using all that the Holy Spirit provides for us through His fruit, gifts, and influence in every area of our lives, whether it is overtly spiritual or "mundane."

PART THREE:

AN OVERFLOW LIFESTYLE

10

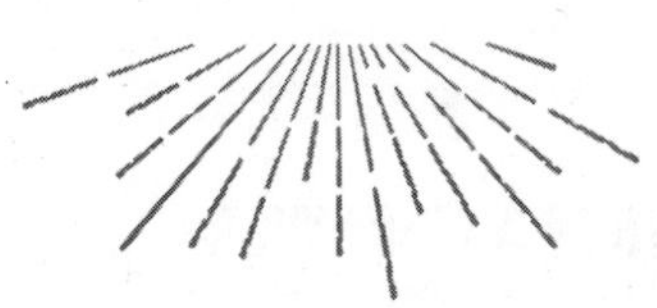

FILLED AND OVERFLOWING

Jesus gave a specific and essential command to His early disciples:

> *Gathering them together, He commanded them not to leave Jerusalem, but to wait for what the Father had promised, "Which," He said, "you heard of from Me; for John baptized with water, but* ***you will be baptized with the Holy Spirit*** *not many days from now.... But* ***you will receive power*** *when the Holy Spirit has come upon you; and* ***you shall be My witnesses*** *both in Jerusalem, and in all Judea and Samaria, and even to the remotest part of the earth."* (Acts 1:4–5, 8 NASB)

It's only with this power from the Holy Spirit that we can give anything close to an accurate representation of (be a witness of) who Jesus is.

OUR NEED FOR AUTHORITY AND POWER

While Jesus was on earth, He gave His disciples authority and power to be able to work with Him in His ministry. (See, for example, Luke 9:1–6; 10:1–20.) In a sense, they were deputized to function under His gifts and authority. But when Jesus ascended to heaven, they needed to receive these two graces of authority and power for themselves.

Authority was given to Jesus's followers in the Great Commission. The authority we walk in is equal to our embrace of His mission, into which, as we have seen, we are *co-missioned*:

> *And Jesus came up and spoke to them, saying, **"All authority has been given to Me** in heaven and on earth. **Go therefore** and make disciples of all the nations, baptizing them in the name of the Father and the Son and the Holy Spirit, teaching them to observe all that I commanded you; and lo, I am with you always, even to the end of the age."*
>
> (Matthew 28:18–20 NASB)

I imagine the disciples had been beside themselves with joy and bewilderment earlier when the resurrected Christ stood before them, giving them instructions to follow for the rest of their lives. (See Luke 24:36–49.) Part of that instruction concerned their mission to go into all the world with the gospel. But Jesus warned them not to fulfill that commission until they had the other grace: power. *"And behold, I am sending forth the promise of My Father upon you; but you are to stay in the city until you are clothed with power from on high"* (Luke 24:49 NASB).

Jesus made it clear that both power and authority are needed to carry out our assignment as His disciples. He made this clear by how He lived and how He trained His disciples in His earthly ministry. And now He reaffirmed this truth in His post-resurrection instructions. It is our responsibility to pursue and receive what God has promised and made available to all believers. Authority comes in the co-mission, while power comes through encounter with the Holy Spirit.

"BE FILLED WITH THE SPIRIT"

> *And do not get drunk with wine, for that is dissipation, but **be filled with the Spirit**, speaking to one another in psalms and hymns and spiritual songs, singing and making melody with your heart to the Lord.* (Ephesians 5:18–19 NASB)

In the Greek, the words translated *"be filled"* are in the present imperative tense, which means that we are to be in a continuous and ongoing state of being filled with the Holy Spirit.[14] Keeping ourselves in such a place enables us to serve well both in and out of season (see 2 Timothy 4:2), with both authority and power, often accomplishing great things without even trying. This kind of lifestyle will sometimes allow the person on whom the Spirit rests to see more miracles happen "by accident" than they ever did while purposefully seeking them.

In discussing the meaning of Ephesians 5:18, Ché Ahn explains that it indicates "Be continually filled with the fullness of the Holy Spirit."[15] I love that. Be continuously filled with the Holy Spirit's fullness. Being continuously filled impacts the people we minister to, but it also affects our own thinking about, attitude toward, and hope for any present impossibilities in our lives. Our confidence level in God soars to an all-time high when we live in an awareness of *Emmanuel, God with us.* (See Matthew 1:23.) Another way to state this is that whatever becomes an ongoing feast for our souls overflows into a feast for all those under our influence.

Of course, Jesus first modeled this lifestyle. Perhaps this is why people could simply touch His clothing and receive their miracle. Jesus

---

14. "What Does It Mean 'Be Filled with the Spirit'?", A Series on the Holy Spirit—Baptism Versus Filling: Part 4, http://helpmewithbiblestudy.org/3HolySpirit/DefBeFilled.aspx.
15. Ché Ahn, "How to Stay Continually Filled and Overflowing in the Holy Spirit," October 21, 2019, The Passion Translation, https://www.thepassiontranslation.com/how-to-stay-continually-filled-and-overflowing-in-the-holy-spirit/.

was continuously filled with the Spirit. He often went to a mountain to pray—sometimes all night. Here is a reminder on how to stay filled: keep consciously before God in worship and prayer. *"Rejoice always; pray without ceasing; in everything give thanks"* (1 Thessalonians 5:16–18 NASB). This approach to life keeps us continually before God with joy, engaging with Him regarding every issue of life, giving Him thanks and praise in the midst of difficulty and mystery. It keeps us under His constant influence.

> ***WHATEVER BECOMES AN ONGOING FEAST FOR OUR SOULS OVERFLOWS INTO A FEAST FOR ALL THOSE UNDER OUR INFLUENCE.***

> *John testified, saying, "I have seen the Spirit descending as a dove out of heaven, and He remained upon Him. I did not recognize Him, but He who sent me to baptize in water said to me, 'He upon whom you see* ***the Spirit descending and remaining upon Him****, this is the One who baptizes in the Holy Spirit.' I myself have seen, and have testified that this is the Son of God."* (John 1:32–34 NASB)

In John the Baptist's experience, Jesus was proven to be the Son of God because the Holy Spirit came upon Him *and remained.* As I described in the chapter "Made to Host," perhaps this could be evidence of our conversion—becoming sons and daughters of God—that we would be a people upon whom the Holy Spirit continuously rests, those who are continuously filled with His fullness.

In the natural world, being full usually means being satisfied. In the kingdom, it's the opposite. (This is another kingdom paradox.) The most spiritually hungry people I know are those who are the greatest at living a lifestyle of being unceasingly filled with the Holy Spirit. They are in constant pursuit of the *more* of God. This does not speak of what they lack or don't have. It's a testimony of the more that is available in Him. There is always more. And only the childlike can see it and pursue it, sometimes with reckless abandon. Perhaps this is what Paul was talking about when he said to *"pursue love, yet desire earnestly spiritual gifts"* (1 Corinthians 14:1 NASB). This is an aggressive, focused, and intentional pursuit of having the realities of the Holy Spirit's nature and abilities flow through us for the betterment of the people around us. The Spirit wonderfully overflows from our lives, not only to believers, but also to those who don't yet know Christ.

BEING FILLED WITH THE SPIRIT

We are surrounded by impossibilities in our world. And yet at the core of the gospel is this declaration: *"Nothing will be impossible with God"* (Luke 1:37 NASB). That's not meant to be a philosophical statement that helps us feel better about the difficulties of life. It is heaven's bold decree that is to have measurable outcomes. It's a declaration that is looking for earthly partners to help bring about *on earth as it is in heaven*. Impossibilities must bend their knee to the name of Jesus flowing from our lips. This must happen, for it is the miracle realm that testifies and proclaims that Jesus is raised from the dead. If there is no resurrection, then we are all wasting our time. If Jesus wasn't raised from the dead, then we won't be raised, either. There is no heaven, no eternity, no life beyond our time here on earth. (See 1 Corinthians 15:14–20.) Without the resurrection, we have permission to live for ourselves. Yet if Jesus was raised from the dead, then nothing matters more—and He was raised!

Being baptized in the Holy Spirit immerses us in the same Spirit who raised Jesus from the dead—the Spirit of resurrection. In fact, we are born again because the resurrection Spirit of Christ comes to dwell in us. His resurrection life becomes our new life. The life of power is the normal Christian life, and it started with the defeat of sin, death, the powers of darkness, and the grave. Jesus pushed this issue beyond what anyone would have asked for or expected, saying that those who believe in Him would do *"greater works"* than He did. (See John 14:12.) And the "*works*" spoken of in that passage refer, without question, to the miracle realm.

Often, when I teach people about this subject of being filled with the Spirit, I hold an unopened water bottle before them and then ask if the water bottle is full. Of course, it is full for the purpose of the sale. But the height of the water is clearly an inch or so below the top of the bottle. So, technically, the bottle isn't completely full. Then I take another bottle of water and slowly begin to pour its contents into the bottle I just opened, asking people to tell me when it's full. It quickly becomes obvious that the bottle really is full only when it begins to overflow. In the same way that abundance in the kingdom is not measured by what we contain but by what we have given away, so it is with the fullness of the Spirit: we are filled with the Spirit only when there is overflow.

Overflow is not only seen in ministry to others through spiritual gifts, acts of kindness, prayer, and so forth. One can always serve people by following the principles of God's Word and be somewhat effective in each of the areas I've mentioned. In other words, I can do these things and still be totally dry and far away from an *overflow lifestyle.* God honors His Word and our obedience, and good things happen. The overflow I'm talking about is more about the felt reality of His presence resting upon us. This affects our countenance. It also affects and/or flows from our being, our presence. I realize that probably sounds strange to some, but consider this: people were healed by being exposed to Peter's shadow. (See Acts 5:15.) Why did this occur? There's no substance to a shadow, but the reality of the kingdom of God reveals this: our shadow will always release whatever overshadows us. Living in the reality of being filled with the Holy Spirit has an effect on our surroundings.

Many years ago, my office was across the street from an organic grocery store that was next to a post office. In the morning, I would walk from my office to the post office, often stopping by the store on my way back to buy items for lunch. I started pausing at the back door of the store to pray before entering. After becoming aware of God's presence upon me, I would enter the store and pick up the items I needed. This became a regular practice. One day, the owner, who had become a friend, called out to me while I was shopping, saying, "Bill, come over here." I walked over to where he was standing in the organic produce section, and he continued, "Whenever you walk into the store, something is different." I don't think I was more spiritual than other believers who shopped there. Nor do I think I was more filled with the Holy Spirit than the others. But I might have been the only one who intentionally waited until the Holy Spirit rested upon me before I entered. This so affected the atmosphere that the owner noticed. I explained to him that what he sensed was the presence of God.

In essence, this manifestation of the presence of God was a fulfillment of the promise Jesus gave His disciples in the all-important verse in the passage about the vines and the vinedresser: *"If you abide in Me, and My words abide in you, ask whatever you wish, and it will be done for you"* (John 15:7 NASB). As I emphasized previously, this verse is the ultimate expression of co-laboring with Christ. As we learn to live in the felt realization of His abiding presence and keep His Word at the forefront of our thoughts and meditations, we can ask for anything, and it will be done. I remind you that God will always have the right to say no to any request that undermines our purpose or identity.

While the idea that we can ask for anything and it will be done may still bother many people, consider this: Solomon was the only one given the *anything-you-want* opportunity—until Jesus came. Now every believer is invited into a relationship with God in which what they pray truly matters. *Anything we ask will be done.* As we talked about earlier, this concept is mentioned four times in John 14, 15, and 16. The Holy Spirit, while not mentioned directly, is the Activator in making this happen. He is the abiding Presence. He makes the Word of God come alive for those who read it so that it becomes the seed of God's nature abiding in us. He is the driving force behind all anointed prayer, as well. The Holy Spirit equips us to have an influence on what happens in and through people, bringing about the fulfillment of the heart of the Father: *"On earth as it is in heaven"* (Matthew 6:10, various translations).

> ***BEING BAPTIZED IN THE HOLY SPIRIT IMMERSES US IN THE SAME SPIRIT WHO RAISED JESUS FROM THE DEAD—THE SPIRIT OF RESURRECTION.***

THE DIVIDING LINE

The phrase from Scripture *"the early and latter rain"* (see, for example, James 5:7 NKJV) helped me to understand a bit about how and why there was such a mighty outpouring of the Holy Spirit at Pentecost as described in the book of Acts, which we have seen in a similar way in the last hundred years or so. Church growth experts attribute the extraordinary growth of the church in more recent times to the Pentecostal outpouring that took place in the early 1900s at the Azusa Street Revival. Eddie Hyatt, in his wonderful book titled *2000 Years of Charismatic Christianity,* shows that people in the church have experienced the fullness of the Holy Spirit for all of the last two millennia.[16] So, this experience and way of life never disappeared. But something happened at the Azusa Revival that brought it all to the forefront again, from the back burner to the front burner.

Unfortunately, manifestations of the Holy Spirit working through believers have been misunderstood by many people in the body of Christ, causing a separation between believers in the church and hindering the power of our witness for Jesus. We see an illustration of this in what happened with the twelve tribes of Israel when they came into their inheritance in the promised land.

Israel was once a nation of slaves. There were perhaps as many as two million Israelites living in Egypt, where Joseph once served as the right-hand man to Pharaoh. Joseph brought wisdom, safety, and much prosperity to that nation. But as new leaders rose within Egypt, the Israelites lost the favor of being honored guests and became the captives of a tyrannical

16. See Eddie L. Hyatt, *2000 Years of Charismatic History* (Lake Mary, FL: Charisma House, 2002).

empire. Yet they increased in number and strength, and God was preparing and equipping them with courage for the perilous journey to come that would be the gateway to their purposeful future.

The narrative of their freedom, led by Moses and Joshua, is filled with some of the simplest yet most profound stories and lessons in all of the Bible. Stories of this nature are very helpful for me because they illustrate, in a very practical way, our journey of walking with God. You don't need a college degree or a special spiritual gift to understand them. They are displayed in plain sight for anyone who has an interest in their own personal growth.

Israel's story is filled with highs and lows, with events both inviting and challenging, as they attempt to take hold of their inheritance of the promised land. The first generation failed to enter this land because of their unbelief. It has often been said, as I wrote earlier, that it was easy to get the Israelites out of Egypt, but it was much harder trying to get "Egypt" out of the Israelites. The Egypt within them was riddled with idolatrous ways that made a life of faith challenging. Unbelief was the outcome.

Imagine being one of the second-generation Israelites in the wilderness. You've been preparing for this moment for forty years. You sense the time approaching when the twelve tribes are about to enter the fulfillment of their dream. But it was not their dream only. As the second generation, they were armed with the same intent and calling as the first generation that initially received the promise. Then, before the people crossed the river into the promised land, two-and-a-half tribes decided they preferred the land on the wilderness side of the river Jordan. It seemed perfectly suited for the vision they had for their own lives. So, they asked Moses for permission to stay and receive that land as their possession, vowing to cross over into the promised land to help the other tribes take hold of their own inheritance with their military support. These tribes did so, and the whole nation stepped into the fulfillment of God's promise.

Nine-and-a-half tribes lived on the promised-land side of the river, and two-and-a-half tribes lived on the other side—a side that became their inheritance. This land was marked by the same abundance and blessing as the promised-land side, so it was not lesser in the sense of being a forsaken land. It had blessing, too. (See Numbers 32; Joshua 22:1–4.)

However, here's the reality the nation of Israel faced: a river divided the tribes. This is the analogy I see for the church today. The church is divided by a river—the river of the Holy Spirit, for so He is called by Jesus in John 7:38–39 (a theme we will explore in more depth in a coming chapter). This river of the Spirit has people on both banks, often in opposition. They generally have two different sets of beliefs and practices pertaining to how the Holy Spirit works today, and they often have two different disciplines and emphases, though both are committed to honoring the name of Jesus. There are those who believe in the Holy Spirit's work in making us new creations in Christ and in giving us the power and wisdom to live for God wholeheartedly, but they think the baptism in the Holy Spirit and the gifts of the Spirit were only for the apostolic age. Then there are those, like me, who believe that the baptism in the Spirit and spiritual gifts and manifestations were given to believers of all eras and are especially needed in the church today. Even though there are major differences in these outlooks and approaches, unity is possible if believers are willing to find common ground and fight for those on the opposite side of the river. The willingness of the Israelite tribes to fight for the inheritance and well-being of those on the other side of the river is what enabled them to fully step into their own inheritance and identity.

Most families have members who think differently from one another. But, in many cases, they all come to the table to celebrate holidays and the victories of life together. Being a loving family and conducting ourselves with honor toward our family members must be the prevailing value of our purpose in life. For only then can we tap into the exponential power that unity provides and that we need. Unity, even in the midst of our differences, is what will help enable the whole body of Christ to be filled and overflowing with the Spirit to make an impact on the world. (See John 13:35.)

TONGUES AND THE BAPTISM IN THE SPIRIT

The dividing point between many Christians is most certainly the baptism in the Holy Spirit, but particularly the manifestation of speaking in tongues, although there are other expressions of spiritual gifts and other manifestations that bring concern to some people. As I expressed in the previous chapter, to speak in tongues is to speak in a language one does not know. It can be a language of either men or angels. (See 1 Corinthians 13:1.) The "unreasonable" nature of this expression has caused many people to reject it entirely, calling those who speak in this way either "mad" or "out of control." There are many great books on the subject of tongues. It's not my intention to attempt to address this topic fully, as the controversy over spiritual languages is not the focus of this book, but I would like to briefly talk about this particular gift of the Holy Spirit. I am a bit sad for anyone who would not desire to speak in tongues in their personal prayers because it is the only spiritual gift listed that has benefits directly for the user: edification, for one. All the other gifts of the Spirit are for the building up of the body of Christ. It is during such times of prayer in the Spirit that we can receive the power we need to proclaim Jesus to the world.

Paul commanded us not to forbid people to speak in tongues. He also expressed his desire that everyone have and use this spiritual gift, claiming that he spoke in tongues more than anyone else. (See 1 Corinthians 14:1–5, 18, 39.) Paul modeled a lifestyle he wished everyone would follow.

There are those who put aside the spiritual gift of tongues as what they call "the least" of the gifts. Although Paul does call some gifts *"greater"* (1 Corinthians 12:31 NASB), it's still strange to me that anyone would say that something given by God was lacking any value and therefore could be set aside. If my children disregarded a gift from me because it was not as expensive as another, we would be having a challenging conversation at minimum. God is the giver of good gifts. Only good gifts.

When we speak in tongues, the Holy Spirit prays through us in either a form of intercessory prayer or praise—such as when the disciples proclaimed *"the mighty deeds of God"* (Acts 2:11 NASB) at Pentecost.

I'm certain that all of us have come to a place where we have prayed about an issue and have run out of words to fully express what's in our hearts regarding the matter. At those moments, we are painfully aware that there is more to say, but words fail us. Praying in tongues helps us at this point because the Holy Spirit prays through us with brilliant accuracy and power.

I'm also certain that all of us have come to a place where we can no longer fully express what is in our hearts for God Himself when we are offering Him praise. Worshipping in tongues takes us out of our place of lack (of insights, boldness, and faith) into an abundance that better represents God's nature. At such times, the Holy Spirit is the One who empowers and directs our worship, making it effective in ministering to God. And both expressions result in answers to prayer and deeper encounters with God through worship, leading to personal edification and strength. As I emphasized earlier, worship is a Holy Spirit-birthed and -directed activity. (See John 4:24.)

The verses about tongues I have mentioned were inspired by the Holy Spirit Himself. Instead of making our discussions concerning tongues be about who is right or who is wrong regarding this issue, perhaps we could keep it intensely simple and emphasize that *the Holy Spirit is a gift*. Gifts are free. There's no earning a gift. Together, let's allow the Holy Spirit to have His way, whatever that might look like.

> ***THE HOLY SPIRIT IS THE ONE WHO EMPOWERS AND DIRECTS OUR WORSHIP, MAKING IT EFFECTIVE IN MINISTERING TO GOD.***

In discussing the issue of tongues, people have asked if being born again and being baptized in the Spirit are possibly one and the same experience. I don't believe they are. In my thinking, being baptized in the Holy Spirit seems to be a second work of grace. For example, in John 20, Jesus breathes upon His eleven remaining disciples and says, *"Receive the Holy*

Spirit" (verse 22 NKJV, NASB). Receiving the Holy Spirit occurs when a person is born again. This couldn't happen before Jesus's death and resurrection. When Jesus told His disciples to receive the Holy Spirit, He was resurrected and ministering to them before returning to heaven to be seated at the right hand of His Father. And it was to that same group of disciples that He said not to leave Jerusalem until they were *"clothed with power from on high"* (Luke 24:49 NASB). So, those who were born again were now told they needed power to be able to complete their assignment. Those are two separate works of grace.

Getting sidetracked by lesser issues has caused the church to fall short of so many things through the years. The Holy Spirit inspired these words: *"You shall receive power when the Holy Spirit has come upon you"* (Acts 1:8 NKJV). And, quite frankly, there are many people who can pray in a spiritual language who do not walk in power. But I never want to use that reality to discount the significance of the gift of praying in the Spirit. Conversely, there are those who don't pray in tongues who do walk in great spiritual power.

Often, the critics of spiritual gifts point to someone who exercises a spiritual gift but whose life is inconsistent with their claims of spirituality. In other words, either that person uses their gift in an improper way, or they claim to be filled with the Holy Spirit but have major character issues in their lives. Such observations are pointless as an attempt to disqualify the importance of the supernatural in our walk with God. If someone tries to play music by the great composer Johann Sebastian Bach, and they do it poorly, we don't blame Bach. The poor job rests entirely on the person attempting to play. It doesn't mean the music is badly written or lacking in beauty and wonder. In the same way, I think that dismissing the need for the gifts because of those who exercise them poorly is one of the ultimate expressions of foolishness. The Giver of gifts is perfect. Both His design and intent are also perfect. We illustrate His lordship in our lives by yielding to Him, often in matters beyond what we can understand. In fact, it is often my surrender in the midst of mystery, more than my agreement with a theory or a doctrinal belief, that displays His lordship over my life. It is our responsibility to embrace our assignment to function in the gifts of the

Spirit, but to learn how to do so in a way that brings all the honor to the name of Jesus.

POWER IS THE PURPOSE

My upbringing was Pentecostal/charismatic, and the traditional approach I was raised with is that speaking in tongues is the initial outward evidence of being baptized in the Holy Spirit. I see good reasons to believe that. I also see reasons not to be so dogmatic on the subject. I heard one of the fathers of the Pentecostal movement say that to emphasize speaking in tongues as the evidence of the baptism in the Spirit is equal to emphasizing getting wet in water baptism. It certainly happens as a byproduct of the experience. And it is a wonderful and necessary gift. But it's not the point. *Power* is. Being clothed with power was the reason behind the command to be filled with the Spirit. (See Luke 24:49; Acts 1:8.) This is why we are not only to be filled but also overflowing with the Spirit as channels of God's power in the world.

POWER AND WISDOM

With the gifts and manifestations of the Holy Spirit, power and wisdom go together. Let us return once more to the example of Bezalel, the first person mentioned in the Bible as being filled with the Spirit. That filling had many profound expressions, but, as we have seen, the primary endowment was wisdom. (See Exodus 31:3.) Wisdom enabled him to be a living example of the creativity of God, with knowledge and understanding. As we've noted, the New Testament version of being filled with the Spirit is for the purpose of God's power resting upon, and flowing through, His people. When God reveals something new about a subject, He doesn't abolish what was previously revealed. Instead, He adds to it, as Jesus expressed when He told His disciples, "I no longer call you servants, I call you friends." (See John 15:15.) Jesus added a dimension of understanding to their relationship with Him. Friendship was a promotion over servanthood. But it would be a mistake to think that those who become friends of God are no longer His servants. Servanthood is what holds friendship in its rightful place. It's our heart to obey and honor the Master that keeps our friendship with God pure.

Likewise, wisdom remains an essential part of life in the Spirit, enabling us to live in a way that represents Him well. Power is the other side of the same coin. Wisdom was never to be removed from the equation; its manifestation in someone's life is still wonderful evidence of their being filled with the Spirit. But wisdom is like the setting on a ring that holds the diamond of power in place. The combination of the two gives a fuller and more complete picture of what it means to be filled with the Spirit.

Here's a simple example of how the two work together in the context of a great move of God: power is what God uses to start a revival, but wisdom sustains it. Perhaps recovering the value of wisdom in all matters of the Holy Spirit will enable us to move forward into the realm of confronting human impossibilities with power while also moving into the realm of *reigning in life* that illustrates more fully the nature of the gospel, lived well on this earth.

POWER AND ENDURANCE

The part of the storyline about the Holy Spirit that people often forget in their pursuit of spiritual power is that the same power that brings about miracles enables us to endure.

> [The apostles said,] "*Therefore, brethren, select from among you seven men of good reputation,* ***full of the Spirit and of wisdom****, whom we may put in charge of this task [the distribution of food to widows]. But we will devote ourselves to prayer and to the ministry of the word."... And these they brought before the apostles; and after praying, they laid their hands on them. The word of God kept on spreading; and the number of the disciples continued to increase greatly in Jerusalem, and a great many of the priests were becoming obedient to the faith. And* ***Stephen, full of grace and power,*** *was* ***performing great wonders and signs*** *among the people.... But some men from what was*

> *called the Synagogue of the Freedmen, including both Cyrenians and Alexandrians, and some from Cilicia and Asia, rose up and argued with Stephen. But* ***they were unable to cope with the wisdom*** *and the Spirit with which he was speaking.... And fixing their gaze on him, all who were sitting in the Council saw his face like the face of an angel.*
>
> (Acts 6:3–4, 6–10, 15 NASB)

In Stephen, we see the demonstration of both power and wisdom as an example of having the fullness of the Spirit. He was performing miracles that Jesus had modeled for His followers and that He had commissioned them to do. And Stephen expressed wisdom that silenced his naysayers, making them unable to cope with his words. His life emphasizes what both the Old Testament and the New Testament teach us about how to live a life filled with the Holy Spirit.

Stephen was a man of the Spirit who demonstrated the miraculous power of God. His impact was transformational upon the entire city of Jerusalem, including many of the Jewish priests. But in the next chapter of Acts, he also dies as a martyr. (See Acts 7:54–60.) God's power didn't bring about the martyrdom, but it did enable him to endure trial, conflict, and eventual death.

The idea of needing endurance is never a fun one because it means things have not happened in our lives in the way we thought they should have or according to how we've been praying. I would imagine that Stephen and his friends prayed for his deliverance. The deliverance didn't come. And as much as I don't like waiting or living in the absence of a miracle, there are very few occasions in life where we get a better way to demonstrate our trust in a loving Father than that one. Living with the conviction that the Father is good, and yet being in the middle of an experience that seems to contradict our conviction, gives us the perfect chance to illustrate faith. Real faith.

I have several friends who have been beaten, shot at, tortured, and/or imprisoned for the gospel. They have faced opposition on every side, experiencing unbearable circumstances of famines, wars, and intense persecution. But in addition to going through these trials, they have wonderful testimonies of God's intervention and deliverance. Such divine interventions don't always come as quickly as—or in the way in which—we might want. Yet they come. The experiences of each one of these friends make it clear that if they hadn't had a life-changing encounter with the Holy Spirit, their *power encounter with God,* they would not have been able to endure.

Faith brings breakthroughs. But faith with endurance brings both breakthroughs and character. And character is what enables us to be trusted with the extraordinary—long-term. The Bible is clear that *those who endure to the end will be saved.* (See Matthew 10:22; Mark 13:13.) Endurance is a necessary expression of our faith. Power brings miracles, but sometimes power enables us to endure until the miracle comes.

For those who have never been baptized in the Holy Spirit, let me encourage you: it is a free gift that enables each believer to represent Jesus more fully. It is not a badge of achievement or something that makes you superior to another. It is simply an immersion into the presence of God that makes boldness, endurance, and miracles a more normal expression of our faith. Because it is free, just ask. Ask Jesus to baptize you in the Holy Spirit. Take time in prayer and worship to honor Him for His promise. Receive it by faith, trusting in His goodness. And then put on your seat belt. You're in for the journey of a lifetime.

11

MINISTERS OF PEACE, BRINGERS OF FREEDOM

It's easy to define biblical terms according to our own language and culture—and completely miss the intention of Scripture. For example, the word *hope* in our society basically means the same as "a wish." But the biblical concept of *hope* actually means "the joyful anticipation of good."[17] It's like the eagerness of children on Christmas morning before they've opened their gifts. They are already excited and thankful. Hope gives us the permission to enjoy the emotional, mental, and spiritual benefits of an

17. *Strong's*, G1680, Blue Letter Bible Lexicon, https://www.blueletterbible.org/lexicon/g1680/kjv/tr/0-1/.

answer to prayer before it happens, as though it has already occurred. For this reason, we can *"rejoice always; pray without ceasing;* [and] *in everything give thanks"* (1 Thessalonians 5:16–18 NASB). When there is real hope, rejoicing in anticipation of an answer is logical. *"Faith is the substance of things **hoped** for"* (Hebrews 1:1 NKJV). Faith grows in an atmosphere of hope.

In this chapter, we're going to look at one of my favorite words in the Bible, *shalom*, or "peace," and how peace is a central characteristic of the Holy Spirit and the effect of His presence in our lives. We often miss this reality because our culture has distorted our perceptions of the biblical meaning of this word as well.

DEFINING PEACE

Shalom is about as big a word as exists in all of Scripture. It basically means "anything one could desire." That's probably a little excessive on my part, although not by much. I'll explain what I mean, but first let's take a look at the most common definitions of peace from our culture.

In our world, *peace* is usually defined in relation to the absence of something. For example, a primary definition is that peace is "the absence of war." And if that were the only meaning of the biblical promise of peace, most of us would be satisfied, myself included. I hate war. Similarly, *peace* conveys an atmosphere where there is no conflict. Perhaps you've walked into a home, and although it was quiet, it was not peaceful because you could feel conflict in the air. Even in the silence, discord was palpable. *Peace* is also often defined as a lack of noise. It is common to hear people say, "Oh, I love this place. It's so quiet and peaceful." So, quietness is often equated with peace.

These are incomplete definitions in part because they focus on what is missing rather than what is present. But within the kingdom of God, the definition of *peace* is different in that peace is "the presence of Someone." It *is* Presence. The implication is that whenever God is with me, I can have peace—no matter what. In the midst of gunfire, bombs dropping, and chaos all around me, I can have peace. It is also true that I can have peace in the busiest subway in New York City, with all the noise, the crowds, and the pushing and shoving. None of that can remove the Prince of Peace from me. In the same light, I have sat across the table from someone who was extremely unhappy with me, accusing and belittling me, and yet I felt peace because God was there. I'm certainly not saying that I had peace because I was perfect. I simply had peace because God was present, and I was aware of Him. He was there for me. As the psalmist wrote, "*You will keep him in perfect peace, whose mind is stayed on You, because he trusts in You*" (Isaiah 26:3 NKJV).

What a great promise! Perfect peace comes through trusting Him, and trusting Him is the result of where I have placed my thoughts. Considering God, dwelling on Him, and living with an awareness of Him keeps me in a place where perfect peace is possible because He is the only one worthy of my trust.

Returning now to my definition of *shalom* as "anything one could desire," this word covers just about anything one could legitimately desire in Christ. *Shalom* essentially means "completeness," "harmony," "success," "prosperity," "health," "wholeness," "fulfillment," and "well-being."[18] It is that which satisfies the soul of a person because it is the abundance of God's nature and presence in their life. It is an inner-person blessing in that it touches the mind, the emotions, and the spirit of a person. But it also has an effect on the outer world, much as is described in the *prosperity of soul* passage in 3 John that we will explore later in this book. It basically means that abundance on the inside of a person helps to make abundance on the outside possible. Many people reject the teaching of the blessing of the Lord on a person because of the fact that Jesus suffered. And yet Jesus is the One who said He'd give us a hundred times as much as what we left to follow Him, "*with persecutions*" (Mark 10:30, various translations). The last phrase about persecutions is to keep us humble in the blessing and help us make sure we don't put this promise off into the millennial age. Such external blessings include good health (see 3 John 1:2) and financial prosperity. These outcomes are not central pursuits or goals for the believer, but they make wonderful rewards.

18. *Strong's*, G7965, Blue Letter Bible Lexicon, https://www.blueletterbible.org/lexicon/h7965/kjv/wlc/0-1/.

Here is another wonderful definition of the Hebrew word for "peace":

> Shalom describes the "realm where chaos is not allowed to enter" (Hanson, 347), chaos being understood as sickness, war, social strife, or the violation of the covenant.[19]

Consider this description of the word *peace* in light of Jesus's being the Prince of Peace and the assignment we all have of being *peacemakers.* We carry the gospel of the kingdom of God, in which no chaos dwells. There is no sickness, war, social strife, or chaos of any kind in heaven. The effects of the spiritual world are to be felt and realized here and now in the physical world by peacemakers. The following passage is a description of Jesus, the Prince of Peace, and what His effect will be on humanity:

> *"The **Spirit of the Lord GOD is upon Me**, because the LORD has anointed Me to preach good tidings to the poor; He has sent Me to heal the brokenhearted, to proclaim liberty to the captives, and the opening of the prison to those who are bound; to proclaim the acceptable year of the LORD, and the day of vengeance of our God; to comfort all who mourn, to console those who mourn in Zion, to give them beauty for ashes, the oil of joy for mourning, the garment of praise for the spirit of heaviness; that they may be called trees of righteousness, the planting of the LORD, that He may be glorified." And they shall rebuild the old ruins, they shall raise up the former desolations, and they shall repair the ruined cities, the desolations of many generations.... But **you shall be named the priests of the LORD**, they shall call you the servants of our God. You shall eat the riches of the Gentiles, and in their glory you shall boast.* (Isaiah 61:1–4, 6 NKJV)

In Luke 4, Jesus quoted the first several verses of this passage as He announced the beginning of His ministry. But the last few verses are to be accomplished by those who follow Him. How do we know this? Notice the words *"you will be named the priests of the LORD."* Exodus 19 also prophesied that the day would come when God's people would be called *"a kingdom*

19. "Peace (in the Bible)," *Encyclopedia.com*, https://www.encyclopedia.com/religion/encyclopedias-almanacs-transcripts-and-maps/peace-bible, accessed February 5, 2024.

of priests" (verse 6), or the priests of the Lord. But it was Peter who said, "*You **are**...a royal priesthood, a holy nation*" (1 Peter 2:9 NKJV, NASB). The Old Testament writers said the day was coming when all of God's people, not just the tribe of Levi, would be considered "priests unto the Lord." But Peter was the one to announce, in effect, "Today is the day!" All of God's people are priests unto the Lord. And it's the priests of the Lord who help to bring about the manifestation of the Spirit of the Lord in measurable ways in the practical areas of life. And it's the ones who have been healed and restored because of the work of the Spirit of God who help to rebuild ruined cites.

The Holy Spirit, qualifying us for priestly ministry, connects us to the final portion of the above passage from Isaiah: "*They shall rebuild the old ruins, they shall raise up the former desolations, and they shall repair the ruined cities, the desolations of many generations.*" In Jesus, the Holy Spirit has raised up whole new generations of people who, like their Master, give place to the Spirit of God for the purpose of seeing healing and restoration come to the broken parts of life. This is how we see the restoration of true peace in our world. What we are reading here is the result of peacemakers, brokers of Presence, having their influence on society. And that influence comes *only* by the Spirit of the Lord resting upon us as He did upon Jesus. That being said, peacemakers are those who host the Spirit of God well, with great hope and vision for what could be, unwilling to yield to the inferior expectations of religious form and routine. This is what Spirit-filled believers look like: they are at war with chaos—everywhere it attempts to influence life around them. Peace is brokered into this world by God's people who live under His covenant, are overwhelmed by His Presence, and embrace His mission. This is what it means to *be led by the Spirit*.

> ***ABUNDANCE ON THE INSIDE OF A PERSON HELPS TO MAKE ABUNDANCE ON THE OUTSIDE POSSIBLE.***

JESUS, THE PRINCE OF PEACE

Remember that Jesus walked into the room where the disciples were fearfully hiding after His death, and He released peace over them. (See John 20:19–22.) Once again, *peace* means "where chaos is not allowed to enter." *Chaos* is an all-inclusive word for everything that is broken here on earth that doesn't exist in heaven. Jesus released this peace. Or, should I say, Jesus released "Him," the Holy Spirit. And the lordship of Jesus, manifested in the presence of the Holy Spirit, brought about peace and freedom to eleven fear-filled followers of Jesus. He then said they were to do the same thing the Father had sent Him to do: reveal the Father and release the Holy Spirit—in this case, manifested as *peace*.

Earlier, Jesus had released peace over a life-threatening storm that was battering the boat in which He was traveling with His disciples. He had been sleeping through this storm, and the disciples thought He didn't care about their dangerous situation. (See Mark 4:36–40.) Think about it: Jesus released peace over a storm during which He had slept undisturbed. In other words, He released peace over a storm He had peace in. Any storm that we can sleep through, we have authority over. If you have peace within you, it will influence the nature of the world around you. If you have peace, you can share it.

ULTIMATE PEACE AND FREEDOM

So often, people think they are free and at peace (absent of conflict or chaos) whenever they have the ability to do as they please. Money, for example, is power. And those in power feel free. People who win a large lottery prize or have a huge signing bonus often feel this way: they can buy anything, go anywhere, and not be accountable to anyone. And yet some of the saddest people on the planet are those in that position, who liberally buy and buy—but have no peace. They have no freedom.

> *For you, brethren, have been called to liberty; only* ***do not use liberty as an opportunity for the flesh****, but through love serve one another....*

> *I say then: Walk in the Spirit, and you shall not fulfill the lust of the flesh. For* ***the flesh lusts against the Spirit,*** *and the Spirit against the flesh; and these are contrary to one another, so that* ***you do not do the things that you wish.*** *But if you are led by the Spirit, you are not under the law.* (Galatians 5:13, 16–18 NKJV)

Those who follow fleshly pursuits instead of kingdom pursuits are actually at war against the Spirit of God. The above passage was not written to the Hollywood elite, the politicians, or the CEOs of this world. It was written to the church. And the warning is that if we give in to the desires of the flesh, it puts us at war with the One who would use us to bring freedom to other people and restoration to cities: the Holy Spirit. God is a builder. And it is in His heart to restore broken humanity—not just to a place of forgiveness (out of the red) but also to a place of restoration (into the black), illustrating the plan of God.

We need the Holy Spirit, demonstrating the absolute lordship of Jesus, in order to experience and live in true freedom. The implication is that it is actually surrender that brings us into freedom. That's because freedom is not the ability to do what you want. It's the ability to do what is right. And some of the most powerful people on the planet are unable to do what is right. They regret taking drugs. They regret cheating on their spouse. Regret fills their lives because they are addicted to a form of freedom that takes the life of its possessors. But freedom in Christ changes everything for the better.

> *The* ***Spirit of the Lord GOD is upon Me,*** *because the LORD has anointed Me to preach good tidings to the poor; He has sent Me to heal the brokenhearted, to* ***proclaim liberty*** *to the* ***captives,*** *and the* ***opening of the prison*** *to those who are* ***bound.*** (Isaiah 61:1 NKJV)

It is the Holy Spirit who sets both prisoners and captives free. Prisoners are generally incarcerated for something they've done wrong; they are guilty. Captives are in bondage because of what has been done to them; they are victims. Freedom comes to both parties as the Holy Spirit has His way. From God's point of view, forgiveness for the guilty party is justice. From God's point of view, bringing the victim into a place of liberty is justice.

PERSONAL FREEDOM

As much as I like the idea of every believer becoming an instrument in God's hand to bring freedom to others, in order to do this, each of us has to first experience freedom and cultivate it as a lifestyle. The goal is that being led by the Spirit, being empowered by the Spirit, being set free by the Spirit in our personal lives will open up a way of living in us that forever exposes the inferior nature of every other lifestyle. It will position us to love and serve others authentically—genuinely and with authority. Anytime we serve people out of a place of experience in God, we serve with authority.

We must remember that surrender to God leads the way to personal freedom. Like most everything in the kingdom of God, this seems to be a paradox. In this great lesson, we surrender control of our lives to the Holy Spirit, who then teaches us self-control. We yield our ways to God's complete dominion, only to find that's the place where we are the most free. Free to think and feel without restraint. Creating such a culture of freedom doesn't mean that "anything goes." Being restrained by God from fleshly lifestyles actually leads us to the greatest place of living without restraint.

Many church cultures use intimidation and manipulation in their tool set to get people to do the right thing. I think this approach often comes from a desire to motivate people to serve the Lord with all of their hearts. But it usually comes from leaders who have never learned how the kingdom of God actually works. These leaders often act like sheepdogs rather than shepherds. Sheepdogs *drive* the sheep to where they should be. Shepherds *lead* them. Driving the people of God to be involved in more church activities is not the same as leading them in a Christlike lifestyle. (Let me comment here that I do believe there is a place for discipline in the church, as there is in the home. But, often, an effort to control others gets passed off as good leadership.)

Whether it's in the church or our homes, living in freedom is necessary for us to become all that God intended. Our development is stunted in a controlling culture. For example, a fish in captivity will only grow to the size its fish tank can support. A shark that will grow to eight feet in length in open waters will grow to no more than eight inches in the average fish tank. Religious cultures will shout and celebrate the eight-inch shark for its beauty and swiftness, often ignorant that God designed the shark to be eight feet long. Only freedom—the kind the Holy Spirit brings—creates the room for that kind of development.

When the church I serve began to significantly increase in number, the staff asked me how we were to build a big church. They were interested in how to construct a large ministry. I told them I wasn't interested in building a big ministry—I just wanted to build *big people*. For me, big people are not those with the biggest titles. They are the freest ones: free from their past, free to fulfill personal dreams, free to give themselves generously to those under their influence.

> ***BEING LED BY THE SPIRIT, BEING EMPOWERED BY THE SPIRIT, BEING SET FREE BY THE SPIRIT IN OUR PERSONAL LIVES WILL OPEN UP A WAY OF LIVING IN US THAT FOREVER EXPOSES THE INFERIOR NATURE OF EVERY OTHER LIFESTYLE.***

CREATING A CULTURE OF RISK

To become truly free, we must pursue excellence rather than perfectionism. Perfectionism is religion (form without power). Excellence is kingdom. The burden of perfectionism is unrelenting and never satisfied. Often, we bring perfectionistic thinking into our homes and churches, believing that this approach is how we prove our devotion to Christ. It's not. Perfectionism is the opposite of freedom. Let that sink in. In a culture of freedom, people must be free to fail or to not succeed in the way they intended.

This is the point where many people seem to find fault with the way of thinking and living for God that I am encouraging here. But when I speak of *failure*, I am not talking about moral failure or abandoning ethics and becoming dishonest. That is never okay. Forgivable? Yes. But never accepted as normal or necessary. Let me explain what I mean by this type of failure by giving some examples.

THE IMPORTANCE OF FAILURE

I'm an Apple computer fan and have been for about thirty-five years. Like all major corporations of this nature, Apple Inc. has two basic parts of their company: (1) manufacturing and (2) research and development. The two branches of this corporation have two completely different sets of core values. For example, manufacturing has a core value of *zero defects*. They do not want four hundred thousand iPhones to be recalled because of flaws. But research and development's core value is that the developers are expected to fail. A lot. "Failure" in this sense would more accurately be described as *finding out what won't work*. If those doing the experiments don't fail, they can't possibly discover the full potential of their inventions or designs. The boundaries that make excellence possible are found on the edge of success, often made possible by discovering what doesn't work.

As believers, we have two basic parts to our lives as well, which we first talked about in chapter 5, "Made to Host." These are the two legs we stand on: character and power. Both legs need to be of equal length, or we will limp. As sacrilegious as it sounds, we don't really want our character to be stronger than our power. And we certainly don't want our power to be greater than our character.

The realm of character is the manufacturing branch of the church, where we want zero defects. Again, it is the *Holy* Spirit who lives within us, so holiness must become evident in how we do life. Purity in our lifestyle—in our thoughts, ambitions, and behavior—must be pronounced. Ministry/power is the research and development branch of the church. To grow in serving the Lord and serving other people, especially in spiritual gifts, we are required to accept failure in the same way we expect a child to fall when they're learning to walk. After a ten-month-old takes two steps and falls, we cheer, pick them up, and encourage them to try again. Ministry really is a lot like that. And as long as we live in accountability and take responsibility for our actions, this approach to life will enable us to explore areas of life and ministry that we would never otherwise discover. It is religion—that spirit of perfectionism—that keeps so many believers from learning how to serve the Lord in realms of the supernatural. And all ministry that is effective ministry is supernatural in nature. A fear of failure cripples too many people who live with the idea of *no failure* in ministry. They think that this is a sign of maturity, when in reality they have not failed because they have not tried.

TRUE PERFECTION

I've just opposed perfectionism as a religious counterfeit to what God has called us to: excellence. But, in full disclosure, Jesus said, *"Therefore you are to be perfect, as your heavenly Father is perfect"* (Matthew 5:48 NASB). Those who are offended by Jesus's command to *"heal the sick, raise the dead"* (Matthew 10:8 NASB) yet are not offended by "Pray for the sick" (see, for example, James 5:14–15) should have their hands full with the latter commandment alone. Thankfully, all commands given in grace come with the enablement to do what has been commanded.

Perfectionism is a hard taskmaster that keeps us from thriving as followers of Jesus. And the weightiness of perfectionism, which burdens so many, is like a ball and chain that keeps us from the perfection that is found only in freedom. We do not move into perfection by working harder. This wonderful command to *"be perfect,"* which is also an invitation by Jesus, can only be approached through the joy of loving and serving Him well. It is the fruit of true freedom in Christ.

> ***It was for freedom that Christ set us free;*** *therefore keep standing firm and do not be subject again to a yoke of slavery.*
>
> (Galatians 5:1 NASB)

Why are we set free? For the sake of freedom. In other words, freedom is an end in itself and fully satisfies the intention of the Lord for all creation. It is the end goal.

> *For the creation was subjected to futility, not willingly, but because of Him who subjected it in hope; because the* ***creation itself also will be delivered*** *from the bondage of corruption* ***into the glorious liberty of the children of God****. For we know that the whole creation groans and labors with birth pangs together until now.* (Romans 8:20–22 NKJV)

As the people of God become free to think and act in perfect harmony with the heart of God, consistent with our design, creation itself responds. In fact, creation is the benefactor of the liberty we experience as believers. Creation is delivered from futility and given freedom from the effects of sin. We become free to be all that God designed us to be, with the ability to think right, choose right, and live right. God is never more glorified than when those made in His image live to their potential, according to His design. Responding to the inner workings of the Holy Spirit takes us toward perfection every single day of our lives.

As we travel this journey, the Holy Spirit helps us in our weaknesses. That is as good a job description of the Holy Spirit as we'll ever hear, as there is nothing I have been called to do in which I am not weak. He who is power, who is holiness, is longing to manifest more fully through each of us so that Jesus might be seen for who He really is. In all the earth.

THE WORKS OF THE HOLY SPIRIT

Let us keep in mind that every time we see Jesus performing a miracle, we are witnessing the Trinity at work. Jesus only did what He saw the Father doing. That means it was the Father who revealed what, how, and when a miracle should be done. Not only that, but we are also witnessing the work of the Holy Spirit, who was the *dunamis* (power) from heaven resting upon Jesus and flowing through Him that made the miracle possible. And the works testified to who Jesus was:

> ***If I do not do the works of My Father, do not believe Me;*** *but if I do, though you do not believe Me,* ***believe the works,*** *that you may know and believe that the Father is in Me, and I in Him.*
>
> (John 10:37–38 NKJV)

This was a powerful statement. Jesus, inspired by the Holy Spirit, announced to all those who were in the crowd that if He didn't do the works of the Father, they weren't required to believe in Him. A thorough study of the gospel of John will show that when the writer speaks of the works of the Father, he is without question speaking of the miracle realm. Consider this: The prophets foretold of Jesus's coming, creation testified of His coming, the intercessors spoke of His coming, and the angels declared His coming. There are probably more who testified about Him that I missed. And yet Jesus announced that the crowd didn't have to believe any of the credible witnesses that the Father had sent and had used throughout history if this one additional element was not in place: miracles. So Jesus said, in effect, "If the miracles aren't there, you don't have to believe."

> *God anointed Jesus of Nazareth with* ***the Holy Spirit*** *and with power, who went about doing good and healing all who were oppressed by the devil,* ***for God was with Him.*** (Acts 10:38 NKJV)

Miracles were the evidence that the Spirit of God was with Jesus, and they are the evidence that He is with us. I look forward to the day when the church—which has now come to know the same Father that our Elder Brother Jesus does, and which is empowered by the same Holy Spirit that Jesus was—would have the courage to declare to this world, "If we do not do the works of our Father, you do not have to believe our message."

12

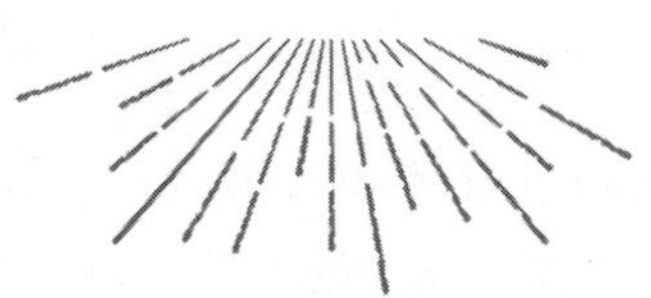

THE RIVER OF THE HOLY SPIRIT

The Holy Spirit and His works are put on display, like a fine art exhibit, throughout the New Testament. We know that everywhere we see Jesus, we see the Holy Spirit working, always to the glory of the Father. In this chapter, we will look at another beautiful description of the Spirit and what it tells us about His presence and work in our lives.

In John 7, the Holy Spirit is described as a river:

> *On the last day, that great day of the feast, Jesus stood and cried out, saying, "If anyone thirsts, let him come to Me and drink. He who believes in Me, as the Scripture has said,* ***out of his heart will flow rivers of living water.****" But* ***this He spoke concerning the Spirit,***

> *whom those believing in Him would receive; for the Holy Spirit was not yet given, because Jesus was not yet glorified.*
>
> (John 7:37–39 NKJV)

It's a very interesting concept that the Holy Spirit is likened to a river in us. Rivers *flow*, affecting everything they touch. They are continuous and ongoing, bringing life wherever they go.

Droughts are devastating natural events that are in stark contrast to flowing water. We have had several years of drought where I live in Northern California. Yet despite this severe lack of rain, the trees along the Sacramento River never seem to know there is a drought; they are clueless. They are growing next to a continuously flowing river that is beautiful and exciting. I have spent many hours on this river, and it is exhilarating. The trees there thrive—and it is the same for all who abide in the presence of God: He is a never-ending river of life.

> *He shall be like a tree planted by the rivers of water, that brings forth its fruit in its season, whose leaf also shall not wither, and* ***whatever he does shall prosper.*** (Psalm 1:3 NKJV)

The river of the Holy Spirit that flows *from* us will first have a transformational impact *on* us. While the challenges of life are always with us, the fact that we're planted by a river has put us in a place of continual influence by the Spirit. I love the outcome: "*Whatever he does shall prosper.*"

PROSPERITY OF SOUL

In the church, the idea of being prosperous in all areas of one's life is a huge issue. Tragically, prosperity is rejected by some believers in the name of humility.

As we began to discuss in the last chapter with regard to peace, when the Holy Spirit lives in us, prosperity of soul is the initial target of His influence. His presence must have a significant impact on our inner world. Let's face it: we have seen that having more money without also having inner health is a nightmare situation. News reports are filled with the tragic stories of those who seemingly "had it all" but overdosed on drugs or killed themselves because it wasn't enough to satisfy them. So, I am not speaking about prosperity according to how our culture usually defines it. There remains a biblical pattern of prosperity that is meant to influence every part of our lives:

> *Beloved,* ***I pray that you may prosper in all things*** *and be in health, just as your soul prospers.* (3 John 1:2 NKJV)

The Holy Spirit-inspired prayer recorded in this verse reveals the will of God: prosperity in every area of life, overflowing into physical health. The fact that such prosperity must be prayed for shows us that this way of living is not necessarily automatic. This desire of the Lord for us must be apprehended in prayer and lived out through a relationship with the Holy Spirit. We know that wherever the Holy Spirit demonstrates the lordship of Jesus, liberty is the result. This freedom is first an inner-man experience, where sin, regret, resentment, shame, guilt, anxiety, comparison, and other negative aspects no longer have a voice or a place of influence in us. Our inner health becomes a stronghold of peace.

When the emotional and mental world of a person is healthy, it affects every other area of their life, from their physical health, to the realms of creativity (free thinking), to wise decision-making, to their financial well-being. For this reason, this prayer in 3 John acknowledges that every part of our life can prosper and be abundant if our soul prospers. At Bethel Church, we have many teams whose primary focus is on ministering healing to the inner man. They testify to the fact that physical healing often follows inner healing.

Psalm 1:3 reads, *"Whatever he does shall prosper,"* and 3 John 1:2 reads, *"That you may prosper in all things."* Both verses reveal the results when the Holy Spirit has a great influence in a person's life. We have noted that the subject of prosperity triggers many people who feel the need to react negatively to this biblical truth. Of course, their reasoning is in reaction to the abuses of some. I get it. But, as I wrote earlier, reaction to error often creates another error. Prosperity can be a result of the influence of the Spirit of God in a person's life. It's our responsibility to find out the purpose of His blessing and use it accordingly. This concept is in the Bible, in the Old and New Testaments alike.

THE RIVER FLOWS FROM US

> *And it shall be that every living thing that moves, wherever the rivers go, will live…, and everything will live wherever the river goes…. Along the bank of the river, on this side and that, will grow all kinds of trees used for food; their leaves will not wither, and their fruit will not fail. They will bear fruit every month, because their water flows from the sanctuary. Their fruit will be for food, and their leaves for medicine.*
> (Ezekiel 47:9, 12 NKJV)

This passage speaks of the effect of the river that brings life to everything it touches, including nations. (See Revelation 22:2.) This is true prosperity. Many would say that this river doesn't represent the Holy Spirit. If not, is it possible that this picture given by the prophet Ezekiel illustrates God's intended use of the River of God flowing from us? Certainly, you'd agree that the river spoken of above could not be more effective than the Holy Spirit flowing through us.

The indwelling Holy Spirit is a river that is to flow from us, bringing life to everything He touches. Perhaps this is what the woman with the issue of blood discovered when she reached out and touched Jesus as He was passing by. (See Luke 8:43–48.) Life flowed from Him. Presence flowed from Him. Healing flowed from Him.

Is it possible to expect that the same life would flow from His disciples? I think so. To expect less is to diminish the work of the cross that qualifies us for all that Jesus taught, modeled, and commanded. Again, "*greater works than these* [you] *will do*" (John 14:12 NKJV) comes into play here. We were designed for greater. We were created for greater. We were redeemed for greater.

> ***THE INDWELLING HOLY SPIRIT IS A RIVER THAT IS TO FLOW FROM US, BRINGING LIFE TO EVERYTHING HE TOUCHES.***

THE RESURRECTION LIFE OF JESUS

I had always wondered why the Holy Spirit wasn't given while the disciples were following Jesus as He ministered on earth. It appeared to me that they really would have benefited from the indwelling presence of the almighty God. They probably wouldn't have caused nearly as many problems or answered so many questions wrong (although the Holy Spirit living in me hasn't kept me from such things!). But the passage from John 7 makes it clear, as discussed earlier, why He wasn't given then: Jesus had not yet been glorified.

We know that Jesus died, was resurrected, ascended to the right hand of the Father, and has been forever glorified. Why was all of that necessary in order to release the Holy Spirit to dwell in believers? To understand this, we have to remember the primary role of the Spirit of God in our lives: to make us like Jesus. Is that not true? He convicts us of sin, leads us, teaches us, imparts to us, empowers us, defends us, comforts us—and the list goes on and on. But everything He does is to conform us into the image of the Son of God, Jesus the Christ. He works in and through us to make us in behavior what we are by position in Christ. This is His primary assignment. And why is that understanding important to our discussion of the Spirit of God not being released until Jesus was glorified?

Picture an artist making a sculpture or painting. They will often use a model and then recreate the image in clay, stone, or on a canvas. And if the Holy Spirit had been given before Jesus was glorified, this Master Artist would be conforming us to the image of the Son of God headed to the cross instead of the triumphant resurrected Christ, forever glorified! The Holy Spirit is conforming us into the image of the glorified Son of God. Perhaps that's part of what is meant by *"Christ in you, the hope of glory"*

(Colossians 1:27 NKJV, NASB). The apostle John saw Jesus in His earthly form for three and a half years, and then he saw Jesus in His glorified, resurrected form in a vision when he was on the island of Patmos, which he recorded in the book of Revelation:

> *Then I turned to see the voice that spoke with me.... One like the Son of Man, clothed with a garment down to the feet and girded about the chest with a golden band. His head and hair were white like wool, as white as snow, and His eyes like a flame of fire; His feet were like fine brass, as if refined in a furnace, and His voice as the sound of many waters; He had in His right hand seven stars, out of His mouth went a sharp two-edged sword, and His countenance was like the sun shining in its strength.* (Revelation 1:12–16 NKJV)

The fact that John was the one who penned the words *"as He is, so are we in this world"* (1 John 4:17 NKJV) adds a bit of clarity and intensity to the statement. Note that we are as Jesus *is*, not as He was. The resurrection life of Jesus, which is the heart and soul of our conversion, must be on display in and through our lives. The Holy Spirit is the Spirit of resurrection who is like a river that is to flow through the life of the yielded believer. This is the Christian life.

"THE ESSENCE OF BEAUTY"

If the Holy Spirit were to have His way, what would the church look like? Like Jesus. Pure and simple. It is for this reason that we are called *"the body of Christ."* (See, for example, 1 Corinthians 12:27.) Jesus is joyful beyond description, is abundantly filled with life, and delights in the wonder of His Father while being perfectly united with the Holy Spirit, who dwells in His people. He skillfully reigns over all things in a way that brings joy to His Father. He is perfect in beauty, in wonder, and in majesty. Around the throne is the continuous decree *"Holy, holy, holy"* (Isaiah 6:3; Revelation 4:8)! Apparently, holiness is a dominant theme of His person, His being. Of all the things that could be declared, such as His worth,

His beauty, or His love, it is His holiness that is proclaimed throughout eternity.

The Bible speaks of *"the beauty of holiness."* (See, for example, Psalm 29:2.) Most of us have been exposed to and/or frustrated by the religious idea of holiness, which is more like self-righteousness or adherence to rules and regulations. As a result, holiness is thought of as restrictive and rigid. Yet true holiness is the heart of freedom. In the previous chapter, we talked about how we may think we are free when we are living fully according to our own design and purpose, but we are never freer than when we are living a holy life. Such a life is called "beautiful." Here is the perfect description of *holiness*: "the essence of beauty." It's tragic to see *unholiness* paraded as *beauty*. It must delight the enemy of our souls to see people fall for the counterfeit. All of the devil's rewards come with a balloon payment. In other words, you can have a reward (pleasure) now, but it will cost you when you least expect it. Partnering with the enemy's works and ways positions us to live in his debt forever. Holiness is the opposite of that. It is permanent freedom because it is anchored in the nature and person of God.

Isn't it interesting that the writer of Hebrews declares, *"Pursue peace with all people, and holiness, without which no one will see the Lord"* (Hebrews 12:14 NKJV)? We'd all be doomed if this required a holiness that was in and of ourselves. But our relationship of surrender to Jesus through the Holy Spirit gives Him the place of influence over our lives to the point that His nature is seen in and through us. He is the *Holy* Spirit. He is the Spirit of Holiness. Responding to His influence is the only possible way for us to live in and experience the holiness of God flowing through our lives.

THE RIVER FLOWED THROUGH JESUS

Even in His earthly ministry, Jesus modeled the victorious life that would be common after His resurrection. He healed the sick before making the payment for their healing by the stripes He bore, mentioned in Isaiah 53:

> *Surely He has borne our griefs and carried our sorrows; yet we esteemed Him stricken, smitten by God, and afflicted. But He was wounded for our transgressions, He was bruised for our iniquities; the chastisement for our peace was upon Him, and by His stripes we were healed.*
> (Isaiah 53:4–5 NKJV)

Interestingly, the Hebrew words translated "*griefs*" and "*sorrows*" are literally "sicknesses" and "pains," respectively.[20] In fact, when Jesus quoted this passage in Matthew 8:17 (NKJV), He actually used the words "*infirmities*" and "*sicknesses.*"[21] The prophet Isaiah declared there would be a transaction that would make healing available and free. It is interesting to note that all of the healings and miracles that Jesus performed occurred before His sufferings. It reminds me of when my wife and I would take our children with us when we went grocery shopping. They would be in the cart as we piled in the groceries. But we would often go down the ice cream aisle first, grab ice cream bars for them, and let them eat the ice cream while we shopped. It kept them happy, which in turn kept us happy. In reality, they were eating something that wasn't paid for. We would simply put the wrappers in the cart and pay for the ice cream before we left the store. What Jesus did is similar. Everyone He ministered to was healed, and He paid for their healings before leaving "the store" (this earthly realm).

Let's return to the account of the woman with the issue of blood, who had borne this affliction in her body for many years. No physician could help her. But then she heard about Jesus, who knew no impossibility. Even though, due to this affliction, the woman was supposed to keep away from the public, she risked scrutiny and scorn from the crowds to access the miracle that was before her. While everyone was pressing in close and touching Jesus, she alone saw what was available to her in that touch. Her perception gave her access to the miracle. As soon as she accessed it, Jesus stopped and said that someone had touched Him. The crowd, including the disciples, couldn't understand

---

20. "Isaiah 53:4," NASB Lexicon, Bible Hub, https://biblehub.com/lexicon/isaiah/53-4.htm.
21. *NKJV Spirit-Filled Life Bible*, 1032.

why He would make such a statement because the most obvious thing in that moment was the crowd pressing in to be close to Jesus. And yet Jesus recognized power flowing from Him. That's the river. That's the Spirit of the living God that flowed from Him. And the woman was healed.

Most of us would never recognize the presence of God flowing from us. But Jesus did, which tells me He lived with a consciousness of the indwelling Holy Spirit. Developing an awareness of Him is one of our greatest privileges and responsibilities. Such a moment is not for show. It's not to gain recognition so we'll be seen as a powerful person. It is the normal Christian life—a life where the River flows from us.

One of the ways I describe it is like this: The Holy Spirit is in you—and He wants out! He is in us as a river, not a lake. Rivers flow and alter the geography around them. It's not that He flows from us and is no longer with us. That's impossible because Jesus promised never to leave us. (See John 14:16–18.) Jesus is eternal and unlimited. The Scriptures say of Him that He had the Spirit without measure. (See John 3:34.) It's the same for each of us who have received the gift of the indwelling Holy Spirit.

As we cooperate with the Spirit, He can flow from us freely, impacting every room we enter, every situation we give our attention to. This is the character of the life of someone filled with the Holy Spirit. This is the life of ministry, for in ministry we are actually releasing the presence of God into broken situations.

> *AS WE COOPERATE WITH THE SPIRIT,*
> *HE CAN FLOW FROM US FREELY,*
> *IMPACTING EVERY ROOM WE ENTER,*
> *EVERY SITUATION WE GIVE OUR ATTENTION TO.*

THE RIVER FLOWED THROUGH THE APOSTLES

The river that flowed through Jesus was meant to flow through those who follow Him. The disciples, turned apostles, were the first to experience this wonder. I'm still amazed at Peter's confidence in what he carried. When he spoke to a man who had been lame since birth, he knew he possessed the miracle power of God that was within him and was about to flow through him:

> *Then Peter said, "Silver and gold I do not have, but* ***what I do have I give you:*** *In the name of Jesus Christ of Nazareth, rise up and walk." And he took him by the right hand and lifted him up, and* ***immediately his feet and ankle bones received strength.*** *So he, leaping up, stood and walked and entered the temple with them—walking, leaping, and praising God.* (Acts 3:6–8 NKJV)

Notice that the release of God's presence, the release of the miracle, was declared or commanded. Peter said, *"In the name of Jesus Christ of Nazareth, rise up and walk."* The miracle was voice-activated.

The disciples were trained in this way of thinking early in their journey with Jesus. It was the model He gave them for all ministry:

> *And as you go, preach, saying, "The kingdom of heaven is at hand." Heal the sick, cleanse the lepers, raise the dead, cast out demons.* ***Freely you have received, freely give.*** (Matthew 10:7–8 NKJV)

"Freely you have received, freely give." What have you received? *Him.* The Holy Spirit.

FOUR WAYS TO RELEASE GOD'S PRESENCE INTO A SITUATION

There are probably countless ways to release the presence of God into a situation, but I know of four main ones. However, let me say again that never are we put in a position where we control or direct God. As I often remind people, He doesn't work for me—I work for Him. And let us never limit the ways in which God may work in our lives or in others' lives but be continually open to the Spirit's leading.

1. THE SPOKEN WORD

The presence of God is released into a situation whenever we say what the Father is saying. That was the experience of Jesus and the example He gave us, which is also to be our experience and example. Once again, Jesus said, "*The words that I speak to you are spirit, and they are life*" (John 6:63). I also remind you of this statement from Psalm 107:20 (various translations): "*He sent His word and healed them.*" The Healer is released into a situation by decree. We see this happen in the New Testament account of the centurion and his slave. That soldier's insight into authority, which he described to Jesus, was remarkable, especially for a Roman. His understanding gave a context for great faith, to which Jesus responded by saying his servant was healed. When the centurion arrived at home, he discovered his servant had been healed the moment Jesus said he was healed. (See, for example, Matthew 8:5–13.)

Perhaps you've been in a dire situation where you were gathered in a room with other family members or friends in fear and uncertainty. Then someone walked into that room and made one encouraging statement, and the atmosphere changed completely. This didn't happen only because the person shared a good idea. Concepts don't change atmospheres. But presence does. As the individual spoke, the presence of the Spirit of God was released into the room, and your outlook on the situation was transformed. A word spoken to bring encouragement sometimes carries the presence of God into a broken situation. Learning to yield to God's heart and mind is the only safe way to discover how to faithfully carry this God-given responsibility.

2. TOUCH

The Bible teaches us about the laying on of hands for various types of spiritual needs. It is sometimes the method God uses to ordain someone into ministry. For example, Moses imparted some of his authority onto Joshua. (See Numbers 27:17–22.) The literal word for the Hebrew term translated as *"authority"* in Numbers 27:20 is "majesty." Even more than that, it "refers to whatever or whoever is royally glorious."[22] Moses gave some of the majesty that God had placed upon him to Joshua so he could lead God's people in a supernatural way as Moses's successor. In the New Testament, the apostle Paul and other church leaders ordained Timothy into service *"with the laying on of hands"* (1 Timothy 4:14 NKJV, NASB). Gifts were imparted to him that he was responsible to maintain. It became the assignment of the Lord for Timothy to keep these gifts active and in constant development. Paul's admonitions to him, such as, *"Meditate on these things; give yourself entirely to them, that your progress may be evident to all"* (1 Timothy 4:15 NKJV), reveal Timothy's responsibility to manage what he had been given through the ministry of the church leaders.

The laying on of hands is also a practical way to impart a healing. Jesus said about those who believe in Him, *"They will lay hands on the sick, and they will recover"* (Mark 16:18 NKJV, NASB). Touching someone in Jesus's name is more than a symbolic act. Through the laying on of hands, we impart what we actually have to give: the presence of the Holy Spirit.

There are also biblical examples of Jesus being touched by someone who was seeking healing instead of His doing the touching Himself. This occurred not only with the woman who had the issue of blood but also with others who touched the hem of Jesus's garment. (See Matthew 14:34–36; Mark 6:56.). Additionally, people were healed or delivered after touching articles of clothing that the apostle Paul had worn. (See Acts 19:11–12.) Again, touching the clothing of Jesus or Paul was much more than a symbolic act. The Spirit of God will often saturate a cloth, similar to cloth being soaked in a natural river. The miracle anointing on a person's life can be received by a simple touch of the clothing in an act of faith. Each touch gives people access to a measure of presence that is in the cloth because it was touched by an anointed person.

Perhaps the most extreme example of this phenomenon is when the apostles laid hands on people who were then baptized in the Holy Spirit. (See, for example, Acts 8:14–17.) Such an encounter with God that forever

22. *NKJV Spirit-Filled Life Bible*, 606.

marked their lives with the power of the Holy Spirit was the result of a touch. Think of it: the power and presence of God were released through the obedient touch of another human being. This testifies of the greatness of God, not the greatness of any individual. At the end of the day, all of these expressions are by the grace of God.

3. A PROPHETIC ACT

Prophetic acts are found throughout Scripture, but they are often overlooked or considered incidental. *Prophetic act* is not a biblical term. It is simply a descriptor to help us identify something through which God flows. It is an act in the natural that releases something in the spiritual. And it is almost always unconnected logically to the intended outcome. In 2 Kings, we find an example of a prophetic act in an incident involving Elisha and the sons of the prophets. Elisha had accompanied the other prophets as they cut down trees to build a dwelling where all of them could live. The head of the axe that one of the prophets was using fell off its handle and sank into the nearby Jordan River. *Lost.* This son of the prophets was particularly distressed by what happened because he had borrowed the axe. The desire in this illustration was the recovery of the axe head. The prophet appealed to Elisha, who asked him where the axe head had fallen, then cut off a branch and threw it into the water, after which the lost axe head floated to the surface so it could be retrieved. You might throw branches into the water until Jesus returns and never again get a sunken axe head to float to the surface. Throwing the branch into the water didn't make the axe head swim. It was Elisha's following the leading of God's Spirit in a prophetic act that led to the miracle. (See 2 Kings 6:1–7.)

Another great example of a prophetic act is when the Israelites were fighting the Amalekites, who had attacked them in the wilderness. As long as Moses held his arms up in the air, Joshua and his army were winning the battle. But when Moses lowered his arms, they were losing. (See Exodus 17:8–13.) There is no logical connection between an army's victory and the raised hands of their leader. It does us no good to imagine that God will somehow act on our behalf because we're willing to do something unusual or unreasonable and say it's from Him. Obedience is the key on our end of the equation. We must listen to what God is telling us to do and then do it.

4. AN ACT OF FAITH

An act of faith is an action that illustrates our belief and trust in God. Unlike a prophetic act, it is directly connected to the desired outcome. When we were ministering in Weaverville, California, a man once came to the town theater where we held our meetings on Sundays. This man had fallen off his deck at home and seriously injured his ankle. He had crawled into his house and asked his wife to take him to the hospital because he was unable to put any weight on his leg without experiencing excruciating pain. The theater was on the way to the hospital, and the man knew we were meeting there that morning and wanted to see if God would heal him, so he asked his wife to stop there. Our service had just ended, so I was out front talking with people who were on their way home. The man's wife drove him to the curb where I was standing. He got out of the car, and, supporting himself on one leg, he held on to the passenger-side door of the car and explained the situation. I prayed for him at least twice without seeing any progress at all. Then I had an impression that he needed to slowly put weight on the ankle as I prayed one more time. The idea of causing further injury to someone so they could prove their faith was a terrifying thought to me. But if the man did it slowly enough, he could monitor the situation on his own. He agreed. As I prayed again, he slowly put weight on his injured foot until he was able to stand on it without any pain. It was a great lesson for me as I saw that he had faith enough to come to the theater and to trust my suggestion. I actually saw the miracle happen as the coloring and shape of the ankle changed back to normal before my eyes.

In this story, we can see that the action was connected to the desired outcome. The man wanted to be healed so he could walk without pain. Slowly placing weight on his foot was an act of faith that released the miracle.

I've seen this happen so many times through the years where people with broken tailbones sit down hard on their chair, those with bone spurs in their heels stomp their foot, and those who were unable to walk take off running without pain. In the action, the miracle is released. Jesus encouraged acts of faith with statements like *"Rise, take up your bed and walk"* (John 5:8 NKJV) and *"Go, wash in the pool of Siloam"* (John 9:7, various translations). Acts of faith release the hand of God in beautiful ways.

We need to caution people whenever they think their act of faith earns the miracle. People with this mindset often do foolish things trying to prove their faith, and it usually ends in disaster. I will only give someone a direction with risk when I sense it comes from the presence of God, not just as a biblical principle. I know that may sound wrong, but consider this: A widow in Elijah's day was instructed to cook her last meal and give it to the prophet. Her obedience opened up the windows of heaven for her, and she lived in the blessing of abundance following her act of faith. (See 1 Kings 17:8–16.) But it would be wrong for me to go to the people of God and require them to empty their bank accounts and give to the ministry, or perform other similar actions, just because the principle is in Scripture. It's in the Bible, for sure. But I'll never put another person at risk out of a principle. Such a direction must come from the presence of God, the Holy Spirit, and then we must obey.

In this context, it is impossible to separate an act of faith from obedience. It releases the miracle.

Each of these four actions releases the power and presence of God into a situation. When He shows up, He works wonders, and His works are always redemptive in nature.

THE FLOW OF THE HOLY SPIRIT

I've often heard wonderful men and women of God talk about the flow of the Holy Spirit. It's a brilliant way to describe their experience of the River that is in them. Learning to recognize Him and cooperate with Him is one of the great highlights or privileges in life. We fall into error and make mistakes when we think we can control or direct His activities, as though we were in charge. The Holy Spirit will not be controlled by us. Yet, as I have expressed throughout this book, an equally disturbing failure is to pull ourselves out of a position to be used by God to help bring about the desires of His heart: miracles, signs, and wonders. To disqualify ourselves from what He has qualified us for is one of the ultimate expressions of self-will and arrogance. Spiritual breakthroughs happen through those who obey His voice. And those who hear His voice well enough to obey it are usually those who believe these breakthroughs are His desire in the first place and seek His face to bring them about. They are usually the ones willing to take whatever risk is necessary to see God's will manifested on earth as it is in heaven. Another way to put it is that merely a *willingness* to hear and obey God's command is often not enough. That puts the responsibility entirely on God's shoulders to do something He has already revealed in the Scriptures as being His will. In my experience, being able to hear His command is often the result of seeking His face for a greater measure of breakthrough. It's often far more than seeking God for a specific situation, although that would certainly be appropriate. It is usually the result of seeking God for a greater demonstration of who He is, what He is like, and what He wills through the life of the one seeking His face.

As I mentioned earlier in this chapter, Peter's experience with the man who had been lame since birth was noteworthy. As he and John were walking to the temple to pray, they saw this man asking for money. Peter told the lame man to look at them, and then fixed his gaze upon him. *"Peter said, 'Silver and gold I do not have, but what I do have I give you: In the name of Jesus Christ of Nazareth, rise up and walk'"* (Acts 3:6 NKJV).

It's the same concept that is found in the life of Jesus, who worked through the power of the Spirit. Peter didn't have what the man was asking for. But he did have what the man needed and certainly would have asked for if he thought it was available or possible: healing. As a result of Peter's releasing what he possessed, which was the presence of the Holy Spirit, the lame man walked. Peter released this Presence through decree: *"Rise up and walk."*

So, how do you allow the Holy Spirit to flow from you? Move in faith as best you know how, and do so from a place of compassion. This will create a lifestyle in which, more and more, you will see that He flows from you to others.

Somehow, just living with a consciousness of Him is at least half the battle. Faith and compassion come from the Holy Spirit, so living with an awareness of Him positions us for the victories we long for.

13

MY RELATIONSHIP WITH THE HOLY SPIRIT

This is probably the most intimidating chapter I've ever written. I'm not exactly sure why. I feel a little teary-eyed embarking on this final piece to this book. Here I will describe the adventure of a lifetime, and I pray that you, too, will experience a fuller relationship with the Spirit.

FEARFULLY WONDERFUL

Who is the Holy Spirit, and what is He like? Fearfully wonderful, in every possible way.

I can feel the passionate cry of David in Psalm 51:11: *"Do not take Your Holy Spirit from me"* (NKJV, NASB). I can't think of a more terrifying thought, a more nightmarish experience, than to have the Holy Spirit removed from our lives. Perhaps, for me, this unsettling thought was aided by the videos I watched of healing evangelist Kathryn Kuhlman as, weeping, she expressed her absolute dependence on the Holy Spirit and spoke of her day of complete surrender. She said she could take us to the place and the moment where she gave everything to Him. I think hearing that marked me more than I could have known at the time. I just know the Holy Spirit is the tenderest of all subjects, yet He is not a subject. He is a Person who holds all of life together into a meaningful and glorious illustration of the beauty and nature of God. He is God with us.

Once you realize He really is everywhere, it's embarrassing to recognize how much of life you have lived without an awareness of Him—the obvious One. Especially when you see that His fingerprints are all around us, continuously testifying of God's goodness, beauty, and wonder. The reward of John 15:7, asking whatever you desire, is the result of living with a consciousness of Him and His voice.

A PRICELESS CHALLENGE

Imagine a billionaire coming to you with a challenge. He has in his possession a ring with the rarest of diamonds in its setting, valued at fifty million dollars. The billionaire has this offer: You have to wear the ring for six months without ever taking it off. You can't even remove it to shower. If you are successful in wearing and caring for this ring, you get to keep it. If you somehow lose it, you are indebted to the man for the sum of fifty million dollars. You would lose everything you own. Do you accept the challenge? Most of us would undoubtedly say yes.

So now, if you accept the challenge, let me ask you this: When you are out to dinner, are you aware of the ring? When you shower, are you conscious of what's on your finger? How about when you attend church? Do you keep your hand in your pocket a lot so that people won't ask you about it? What about when you wake up in the morning or climb out of a swimming pool—are you aware of the ring? Most people would say, "Yes, yes, yes."

The same would be true of me. I would always be aware of this extremely valuable ring. I wouldn't be able to ignore it or forget it. And I doubt the novelty would wear off in ninety days or even six months. Perhaps five years of wearing the ring would create a neglectful familiarity with it. But not six months. And yet we have One living inside us who is more valuable and more glorious and obvious than all the wealth in the world. To live unaware of Him is a tragic waste of the potential for connection with God and the activation of affection toward Him.

It's usually only those who have breathing issues who live with an awareness of every breath they take. There's such labor involved that they can't help it. But those who have healthy lungs and breathe normally seldom give a thought to what is natural for us all. Our breathing happens every moment of every day, even while we sleep. I don't consciously think about the fact that I have been breathing all day and all night, and yet I have been.

Similarly, the Holy Spirit's presence is constant. He never leaves. But it is possible, and actually common, for us to live *within reach* of this One but still be *unaware* of Him. For me, my strength in my relationship with the Holy Spirit is my affection for Him. If I consider Him, His nearness, and His nature, my heart burns for Him. It's impossible for me to consider Him and have no response toward Him. It would terrify me to think that I might go so long without acknowledging Him that I could consider His nearness and not be moved by it.

Brother Lawrence wrote the classic book *The Practice of the Presence of God*. In it, he describes his journey to live with a consciousness of the Holy Spirit's presence every moment of every day. And while, by his own admittance, he never achieved perfection in this area, he did constantly improve in it. He finally got to the place where being aware of Him while washing the pots and pans was as deep an encounter and fellowship with God as when he was in the chapel praying.

UNCONSCIOUSLY CONSCIOUS

Waking up to the reality that the presence of the almighty God is not only with us but also dwells in us marks our consciousness in a way that changes everything about our lives.

I am a steward of so much: family, friendships, gifts, insights, opportunities, favor, and about a thousand other things. Each area must be cultivated in reverence and for the glory of God. But there's no greater assignment than stewarding God Himself. He gave Himself to us as an inheritance. He is the fifty-million-dollar ring that I can't become too familiar with, or I will lose my awe of. It's the awe that enables me to clearly see the God who is with me.

The first chapter of Genesis says that there was *"the evening and the morning"* (verse 5 NKJV), which made up the first day. That means our day actually begins at night. And most of us would have better days if we had better nights.

I start and end my day by reading the Bible. After reading at night, I lie down and turn my heart of affection toward the Holy Spirit. It's not a time when I want to sing worship songs or intercede for the nations. I want to sleep. But I do want to sleep *in the embrace of the Spirit of God.* It's a simple time when I live in an awareness of Him and allow that to be the anchor of my soul. The Holy Spirit is such a lover that He responds so quickly to the affections of my heart for Him. His nearness is too wonderful to miss and live unaware of. If I wake up in the night, I try to reactivate my awareness of Him and once again come into the embrace of the presence of the Spirit of God. It is a lifestyle that is possible and surpasses every other option for living.

Solomon said, *"I sleep, but my heart is awake"* (Song of Solomon 5:2 NKJV). The spirit-man is always awake and ready to commune with God, even while our physical bodies sleep. This is a natural state for the believer.

> ***WAKING UP TO THE REALITY THAT THE PRESENCE OF THE ALMIGHTY GOD IS NOT ONLY WITH US BUT ALSO DWELLS IN US MARKS OUR CONSCIOUSNESS IN A WAY THAT CHANGES EVERYTHING ABOUT OUR LIVES.***

RESPONDING TO THE AUTHOR

The Holy Spirit inspired the Scriptures. They were "God-breathed," as some Bible versions translate 2 Timothy 3:16. That is the perfect description because I can feel the life of God come off the pages of the Bible as I read. The Bible is the only book in the world whose Author shows up every time we read it.

Reading *with* the Holy Spirit is the only logical way to read the Bible. This is not to say I understand all that I read, nor is He ready to answer all my questions. But my relational journey with the Holy Spirit is a joy in itself. It is connected to my reading of the Bible. He inspires me and gives me understanding of what is written there.

As I said previously, I will admit that, if I am anxious, I don't hear Him well, even from the pages of the Bible. Learning how to live in peace, away from fear, is a lesson I continue to learn, and I think it is one of the most needed lessons for the church as a whole.

MAINTAINING PEACE

Protecting my peace has been more challenging for me in the last three years than at any other time of my life. I have to be aware of the peace of His presence in order to protect it. Otherwise, I will pick up offense, resentment, regret, or any of the many other enemies of peace and *give the dove no place to rest.* When I realize I am without peace, I have to retrace my steps to see where I left it because I previously had it. It is His permanent gift to my life. As I think through my day, I try to find where I laid down my peace for something like an inferior perspective of a situation. Perhaps it was that phone call where I became so frustrated that I picked up an offense. Maybe it was when I looked at my mail and saw the letter from the IRS. Panic took the place of peace. Or it might have been when I heard reports that a trusted friend had taken a stand against me and was spreading rumors about me. Resentment or the desire for vindication doesn't cohabit with peace. Whenever I recognize the moment or the issue that caused me to lose my serenity, repentance is the absolute key. I never blame someone else for my neglect. I can't control what is done to me, but I can control my response to it. I then confess my sin and recover His gift of peace for my life. It is a gift and can't be earned, so I pick it up from where I left it.

LEARNING AFFECTION

As I look back over my life, I would have to say that my commitment to minister to God as a priest (according to Exodus 19:6 and 1 Peter 2:9) in thanksgiving, praise, and worship was one of the most important covenants I have ever made. It was in response to my dad's teaching on Ezekiel 44:15–31, where the priests were instructed on how to minister in the inner court (to God) and the outer court (to people). It truly changed my life by giving me an understanding of our original design as New Testament believers.

In our ministry to God, we attend to Him. He's not an egotist in need of our affirmation, but because we always become like the one whom we worship, God could want nothing better for us than to become like Him. That's what love does: it chooses the best. This explains why God looks for worshippers, not worship itself.

God's presence comes so powerfully during such times of ministry. David taught us that God inhabits the praises of His people. (See Psalm 22:3 KJV.) It's as though our praise becomes the throne that He sits upon. It is in His presence that we learn to receive, to give, and, above all, to recognize Him. Once again, the Holy Spirit is really the One who leads all true worship because those who truly worship God *worship Him in spirit and in truth.* (See John 4:23–24.)

Learning God's ways enables us to recognize Him at work in the various and unusual issues we encounter in life. Those who long for God see Him more easily than those who are waiting for Him to invade their space and make Himself overtly obvious. Hunger sees. Faith sees.

Affection for God is a vital expression, and it comes from having an enlarged heart. *"I will run the course of Your commandments, for* ***You shall enlarge my heart****"* (Psalm 119:32 NKJV). Having an enlarged heart is the ever-increasing capacity to recognize God with delight and do whatever He says. In this place of intimate connection, we learn the ways of divine affection. We are shaped by our time in the glory, which is the manifest presence of Jesus.

In this place of affection, an understanding of spiritual things is awakened in us that has often lain dormant for our whole lives. It's not until we enter the realms of God's glorious presence that we discover the atmosphere we were designed to live in. Our inner man sees it clearly and responds with surrender.

Affection leads us to *adoration,* which is a more biblical term than affection. Adoration is at the heart and soul of true worship. Remember that one of the Greek words for *worship* means "to kiss," which clearly emphasizes the intimate connection we were born for.

To offer adoration means to be captivated by the One. To ascend the hill of the Lord with all of life laid down. Time stops. Problems cease. Nothing matters but His heart. Surrendering, pursuing, drawing nearer to the Lord. This is the life of the lover of God.

The Scriptures tell us that *"we love Him because He first loved us"* (1 John 4:19 NKJV). It's important to realize that there is only one place in the universe to find perfect love, and it's in the heart of God. The implication is that I can give away only what I have received. So, being an object of His love, and being conscious of it, is critical to having my capacity for affection opened up. This capacity becomes activated by the love and presence of

God. Learning how to burn with affection for Him is born out of a lifestyle of worship. At least, this has been true for me. For so many years, turning my heart to Him while asking for nothing but simply to love Him well has been my dream and my pursuit.

When we speak of learning something, we often think of outlines, steps, points, or principles. And while I may eventually use such resources, my heart is where my primary learning is taking place. Things are being reworked in me so I can learn how to love God well. I am being trained and equipped for such a task.

> *TO OFFER ADORATION MEANS TO BE CAPTIVATED BY THE ONE. TO ASCEND THE HILL OF THE LORD WITH ALL OF LIFE LAID DOWN. TIME STOPS. PROBLEMS CEASE. NOTHING MATTERS BUT HIS HEART. SURRENDERING, PURSUING, DRAWING NEARER TO THE LORD. THIS IS THE LIFE OF THE LOVER OF GOD.*

LOVING HIM WITH SPIRIT, SOUL, AND BODY

Consider this: the psalmist said, *"My heart and my flesh cry out for the living God"* (Psalm 84:2 NKJV). Notice what is expressed in this verse: *"My heart **and** my flesh."* It is possible for the human body (flesh) to reawaken the appetite for the Holy Spirit that we were originally created with. It doesn't happen simply because we try to awaken it. That is beyond human talent or determination. It occurs in a realm that we can only surrender to and yield our way into.

We were already designed with this potential in mind. There's something transformational about being in the presence—the overwhelming presence—of the Spirit of God. It's not one-stop shopping or five minutes of singing "Amazing Grace" that brings change. Transformation involves a continuous yielding to the glory of the almighty One. It comes in measures and dimensions that must be stewarded for increase. Remember that our going "*from glory to glory*" (2 Corinthians 3:18 NKJV, NASB) was God's idea and plan, and we move into continual increase through our faithfulness to remain in the Presence.

In addition to all of this, we can have our senses trained to discern good and evil. "*But solid food belongs to those who are of full age, that is, those who by reason of use have* ***their senses exercised to discern*** *both good and evil*" (Hebrews 5:14 NKJV). "*By reason of use.*" We consciously practice, with intentionality, to learn from our ongoing experiences in life. Simply being aware of the potential of a moment enables us to learn some of what we'd miss if we didn't enter into that moment and learn all we could from it.

How are people trained to recognize counterfeit money? Only by studying real money. How are we trained to discern evil? Only by studying the real and the good that is God. Becoming familiar with the Holy Spirit enables us to recognize what is false. And please catch this: it's our natural senses that were designed to recognize God—sight, hearing, touch, taste, and smell. God's world and presence can be discerned through these natural tools. Again, this doesn't come from a course or a book but is only activated in the glory. It is only discovered in the surrender we embrace as we worship our way deeper into the glorious presence of the Holy Spirit.

WHERE WISDOM IS BORN

There are those who say you can't be intimate with God and also properly fear Him, an idea they derive from a statement in 1 John 4:18. But this conclusion is inconsistent with the whole of Scripture. Plus, whoever made that inference was probably never married. I loved my wife, delighted in her, and was very intimate with her. But I also had a healthy fear of her, never wanting to violate who she was or to dishonor her in any way. It drew me to her in deeper love and affection.

> ***The fear of the Lord is the beginning of wisdom****; a good understanding have all those who do His commandments. His praise endures forever.*
> (Psalm 111:10 NKJV)

Fearing God is the beginning of wisdom. To fear God means more than having mere respect for Him; it means acknowledging His holiness, righteousness, and power while still living with a full awareness of His love. We see in one of Jesus's parables that the man who misused his talent (sum of money) had a relationship with his lord that was based on a misplaced sense of fear:

> *Then he who had received the one talent came and said, "Lord, I knew you to be a hard man, reaping where you have not sown, and gathering where you have not scattered seed. And* ***I was afraid, and went and hid your talent*** *in the ground. Look, there you have what is yours."*
> (Matthew 25:24–25 NKJV)

There is an unhealthy fear that drives us from a relationship with God, and there is a healthy fear that draws us tenderly to Him. The former is a fear of God's power without a recognition of His compassion and righteousness. The latter is an understanding of His holy nature combined with a knowledge of His love, forgiveness, and acceptance of us in Christ. And it's the latter that leads to life.

Wisdom is the key gift for reigning in life. When we reign from the mind of Christ, it illustrates the coming of heaven to earth and a freedom in living that reveals the heart of a perfect Father. The Holy Spirit is the administrator of such wisdom.

WORTHY OF OUR *YES!*

So, who is the Holy Spirit, and what is He like? He is God. He is Friend. And He is worthy of my *yes* to live with a continual consciousness of His abiding presence while embracing and meditating on all that He says. In doing so, I have the privilege of co-laboring with Him to see the reality of His world shape and define everything around me.

Yes, Holy Spirit, yes!

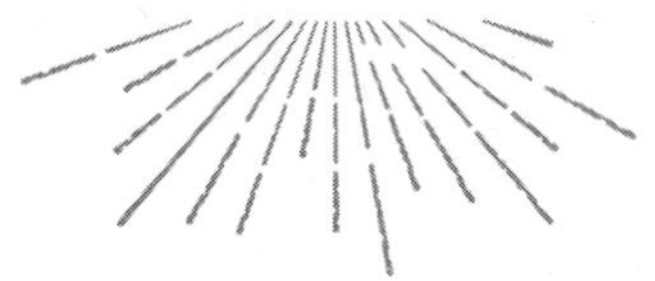

ABOUT THE AUTHOR

Bill Johnson is the Senior Leader of Bethel Church in Redding, California, where he has ministered since 1996, and the cofounder of the Bethel School of Supernatural Ministry (BSSM). A fifth-generation pastor, Bill serves a growing number of churches that have partnered for revival. This apostolic network has crossed denominational lines in building relationships that enable church leaders to walk in both purity and power. Bill is also the popular author of numerous books, including *When Heaven Invades Earth* and *Hosting the Presence*. His priority in life has been to learn how to host the presence of God and minister to Him. He is passionate about seeing the kingdom of heaven invade earth across all spheres of influence, with the wisdom of God displayed through the church, government, education, and the arts. Bill travels extensively to share what he has learned through his experience, with the conviction that the only way to increase what has been given is to give it away.

Welcome to Our House!

We Have a Special Gift for You

It is our privilege and pleasure to share in your love of Christian books. We are committed to bringing you authors and books that feed, challenge, and enrich your faith.

To show our appreciation, we invite you to sign up to receive a specially selected **Reader Appreciation Gift**, with our compliments. Just go to the Web address at the bottom of this page.

God bless you as you seek a deeper walk with Him!

WE HAVE A GIFT FOR YOU. VISIT:

whpub.me/nonfictionthx